ACTION MAN

Mission - Millennium Crisis : Squad Profiles

EDA Undercover Operative - Personal Data

Name:

Code Name:

Age:

Height:

Distinguishing Features:

Specialist Skills   Rating 1-5

Weapons: _____ Ⓐ Ⓐ Ⓐ Ⓐ Ⓐ

Martial Arts:_____ Ⓐ Ⓐ Ⓐ Ⓐ Ⓐ

Survival Training: ___ Ⓐ Ⓐ Ⓐ Ⓐ Ⓐ

Pilot/Flying:_____ Ⓐ Ⓐ Ⓐ Ⓐ Ⓐ

Communications: _____ Ⓐ Ⓐ Ⓐ Ⓐ Ⓐ

Navigation:_____ Ⓐ Ⓐ Ⓐ Ⓐ Ⓐ

Computer Skills:_____ Ⓐ Ⓐ Ⓐ Ⓐ Ⓐ

Name: Unknown
Code Name: Action Man
Age: 30
Height: 6'2"/185cm
Distinguishing Features: Scar on cheek
Specialist Skills   Rating 1-5
Weapons .... Ⓐ Ⓐ Ⓐ Ⓐ Ⓐ
Martial Arts .... Ⓐ Ⓐ Ⓐ Ⓐ Ⓐ
Survival Training .... Ⓐ Ⓐ Ⓐ Ⓐ Ⓐ
Pilot/Flying .... Ⓐ Ⓐ Ⓐ Ⓐ Ⓐ
Communications .... Ⓐ Ⓐ Ⓐ Ⓐ Ⓐ
Computer Skills .... Ⓐ Ⓐ Ⓐ Ⓐ Ⓐ
Notes: ex-elite forces, intelligent, computer literate, inventive & resourceful, reckless, rugged, high endurance, multi-tasking & sense of humour.

£6.99

Your Photo

Virtual Keyboard

1 !	1 '	2 @	3 £	4 $	5 %	6 ^	7 &	8 *	9 (	0)	Backspace
Tab	Q	W	E	R	T	Y	U	I	O	P	
Caps	A	S	D	F	G	H	J	K	L	;	Return
Shift	Q	Z	X	C	V	B	N	M	<	,	
Control	Alt		Ⓐ					Alt			

Notes:

D101262

Please enter your personal details in the EDA database

| INITIATE | COMMS. | MISSION | STATUS | AM2000PDA |

MIC

EDA Secure Channel

Millennium Crisis

Mission Overview

The mysterious VeXus Corporation has been incredibly successful in selling its anti-Millennium Bug systems software world-wide. This ranges from Banks and companies through to the Military and Governments, even Traffic Control...

...such power in one company is very dangerous if it falls into the wrong hands or is abused.

New Mail

INCOMING E-MAIL - SECURE LINK ENCODING

...lam ƏhewmggbEf jEo bC fichƏ ƏBhIemf nhƏ igI khEƏigI hB bgIbPbIƏie DaID ECmC ƏBhIEKDC DaID aifm khIEƏDMB kaƏeC ƏgChIm DamF......uhCD khIEƏDMB kaƏeC ƏBmmn ImThƏemI Dh hgeI BIkhgƏbCm M pΙoEΣBmC nhƏ i 1iIm. m.o. LTTS GhEeI jm fhCD khIEƏDMBC Ghee oh nBhf TT Dh KK. IamI Ghee ghD dghG bn bD bc MKKR hB fhCD khIEƏDMbC Ghee oh nBhf TT Dh KK. IamI Ghee ghD dghG bn bD bc MKKR hB ECmI bg iefhCD kHEƏbGhpo nBhf kiB nB nƏme fIgoimgmD CICDMfC#khƏhdMBC# FbImhC Dh IbB IBlnnbk khƏDBhe kiB iB nƏme fIgoimgmD CICDMfC#khƏhdMBC# FbImhC Dh IbB IBlnnbk khƏDBhe kiB iB nƏme fIgoimgmD CICDMfC#khƏhdMBC# FbImhC

...DECODING ENCRYPTION...

Message as follows:

>>From: Action Man [http://www.actionman.com]
>>Subject: Mission - Millennium Crisis

...The millennium bug is major problem for any company or individual that uses products that have computer chips inside them...
...Most computer chips were developed to only recognise 2 figures for a date. e.g. 1998 would be seen by a computer as 98. When the year changes from 1999 to the year 2000, most computers will go from 99 to 00. They will not know if it is 2000 or 1900 and hence they will crash...
...In the modern age computer chips are used in almost everything from car fuel management systems, cookers, videos to air traffic control centres.
...end transmission

Decode
Receive
Send
Encrypt
New Mail
e-mail

QUICK ACCESS CARD — Reconnaissance
QUICK ACCESS CARD — Equipment
QUICK ACCESS CARD — Mission Zone

ACTION MAN

Mission - Millennium Crisis : Mission Contents

5

The Action Man annual
is published by

Pedigree®

The Old Rectory,
Matford Lane,
Exeter, EX2 4PS.

Hasbro

ACTION MAN

X-TEAM

EDA's Most Wanted - Personal and Psychological Profile - X-Team

File 76514 - X-Team member - Real name unknown

The X-Team is a criminal organisation headed by the infamous Dr. X.

The long term aims of this organisation are as yet unknown, but links have been found to all types of organised crime.

From street crime to industrial espionage the X-Team has done it all.

The X-Team has spread it's evil web across the world. Destroying all in it's path and hatching evil plots of global domination.

It cannot be allowed to go unpunished.

Name: Unknown

Alias: MaXX, X, Spike, Freak Face, Purple Menace

Age: Unknown

Height: 6'2"/1.85m

Distinguishing Features: Spiky purple hair. MaXX has always appeared with his hands and face covered in bandages masking his true identity.

Psychological Profile: His rough exterior conceals a cold calculating criminal mind only surpassed by Dr.X.

Specialist Skills: Rating 1-5

Skill	Rating
Improvised Weapons:	☒ ☒ ☒ ☒
Martial Arts:	☒ ☒ ☒ ☒
Survival Training:	☒ ☒ ☒ ☒
Pilot/Flying:	☒ ☒ ☒ ☒
Communications:	☒ ☒ ☒ ☒
Navigation:	☒ ☒ ☒ ☒
Computer Skills:	☒ ☒ ☒ ☒

Notes: This feared street gang leader has recently joined forces with Dr.X and the X-Team.

Street Fighting specialist approach with Xtream caution

New Mail

INCOMING E-MAIL - SECURE LINK ENCODING
umCCiom8 $ 1am 3m5EC khB@ iBm eiEgkabgo DambB gmG igl
eiDmCD CiDmeebDm Dh ebgd GbDa Dam 3m5EC 0@ikm CDiDbhg.
kiECm8 $ 3m5EC aiFm Q dmI CiDmeebDmC hBjbDbgo Dam miBDa#
DamI iBm fibgeI khgDBheeml nBhf Dam khBm C@ikm CDiDbhg.
ubCCbhg8 $ qgnbeDBiDm EglmBkhFmB iC i 13 kifmBifig igl
bgFmCDboiDm Dam fICDmBbhEC 3m5EC khB@...

...DECODING ENCRYPTION

Mission: MaXXimum Velocity

Message: The VeXus Corp are launching their new and latest satellite to link with the VeXus Space station.

Cause: VeXus have 6 key satellites orbiting the earth, they are mainly controlled from the core space station.

Mission: Infiltrate undercover as a TV cameraman and investigate the mysterious VeXus Corp.

...end transmission

EDA Secure Channel

VeXus Space Station Programme:

The VeXus Corporation is using a Space Shuttle to deploy satellites at an orbit of 260km. The satellite is then boosted up to its orbit 380km above the earth.

MIC

ACTION MAN

Mission Zone
QUICK ACCESS CARD

Equipment
QUICK ACCESS CARD

Reconnaissance
QUICK ACCESS CARD

Mission Data : MaXXimum Velocity

EDA Technical Data - Keyword Search > International Space Station

Space stations have long been seen as laboratories for learning about the effects of space conditions and as a springboard to the Moon and Mars.

In May 1973, America launched the Skylab space station with a Saturn V rocket similar to those that took astronauts to the Moon. Skylab was an orbital workshop and living quarters for three astronauts. Skylab proved that humans could live and work in space.

Assembly of an International Space Station (ISS) began in 1998. The first ISS crew will arrive and the station will be operational by 2000, starting a permanent human presence in space.

One of the main contractors on the ISS project was VeXus Corp. They have recently used the knowledge they gained on this project to launch their own permanent orbital research facility. With a cost in the billions the question remains 'who is funding VeXus Corp?'

+380km
Orbital Location

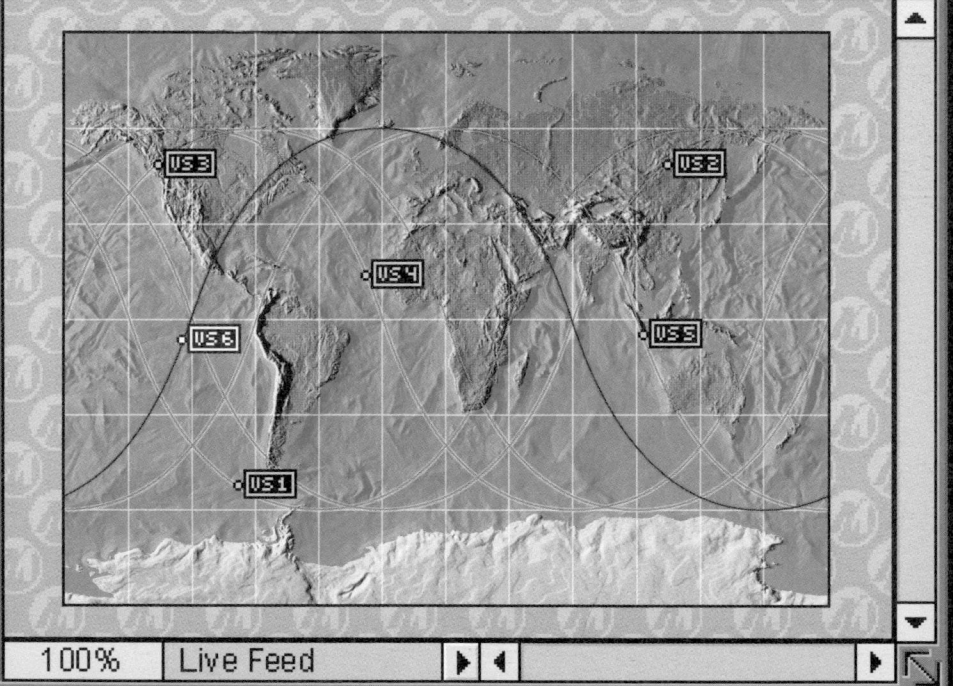

▦ Mission 1 - Satellite Uplink

100%   Live Feed

Orbital Research Facility

Solar Speeder

Working in the field on tough new assignments you have to choose the right equipment. You never know what might come in handy.

Select your equipment from the list below.

- Paraglider
- PDA2000
- Solar Speeder
- Press Pass
- Video Camera
- Heligun
- Space Suit
- Stealth Jet
- Super bike
- 4x4 Jeep

Body shell: Carbon fibre bonded to aluminium frame with kevlar armour

Windscreen: Bullet proof laminated glass

Top speed: 210 mph   **bhp:** 540

Engine: mid mounted V12 with twin turbos

0-60mph: 4.3 seconds   **0-100mph:** 6.2 seconds

Weapons: 2x Multipurpose Sidewinder missiles
             2x 16mm machine guns

Navigation: GPS (Global Positioning System)

R&D asked if you could return this all in one piece!

Briefed

Equipped

Accept Mission

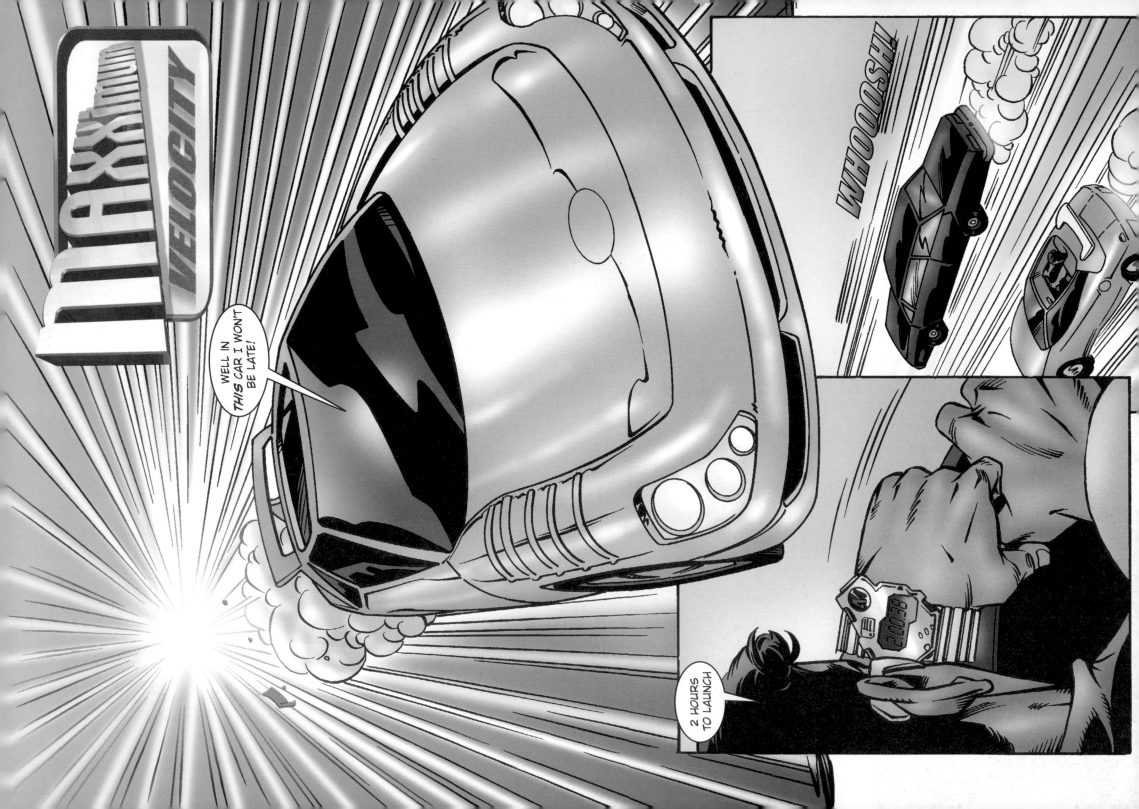

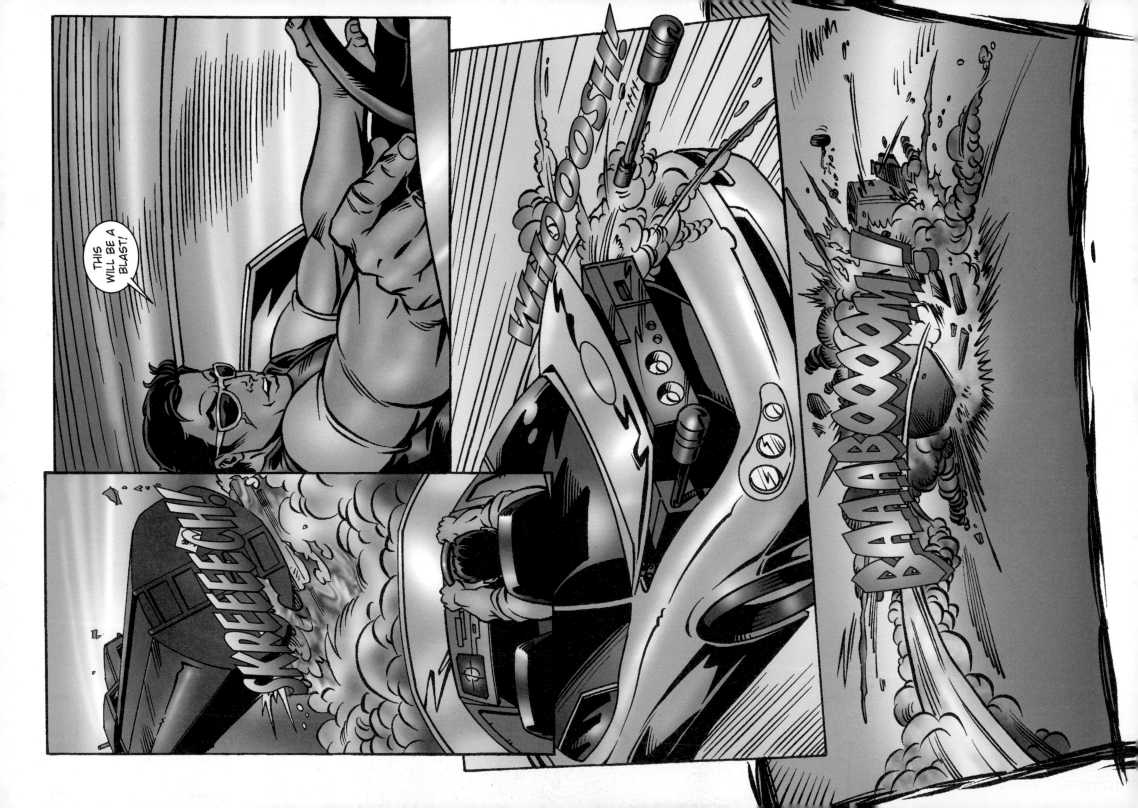

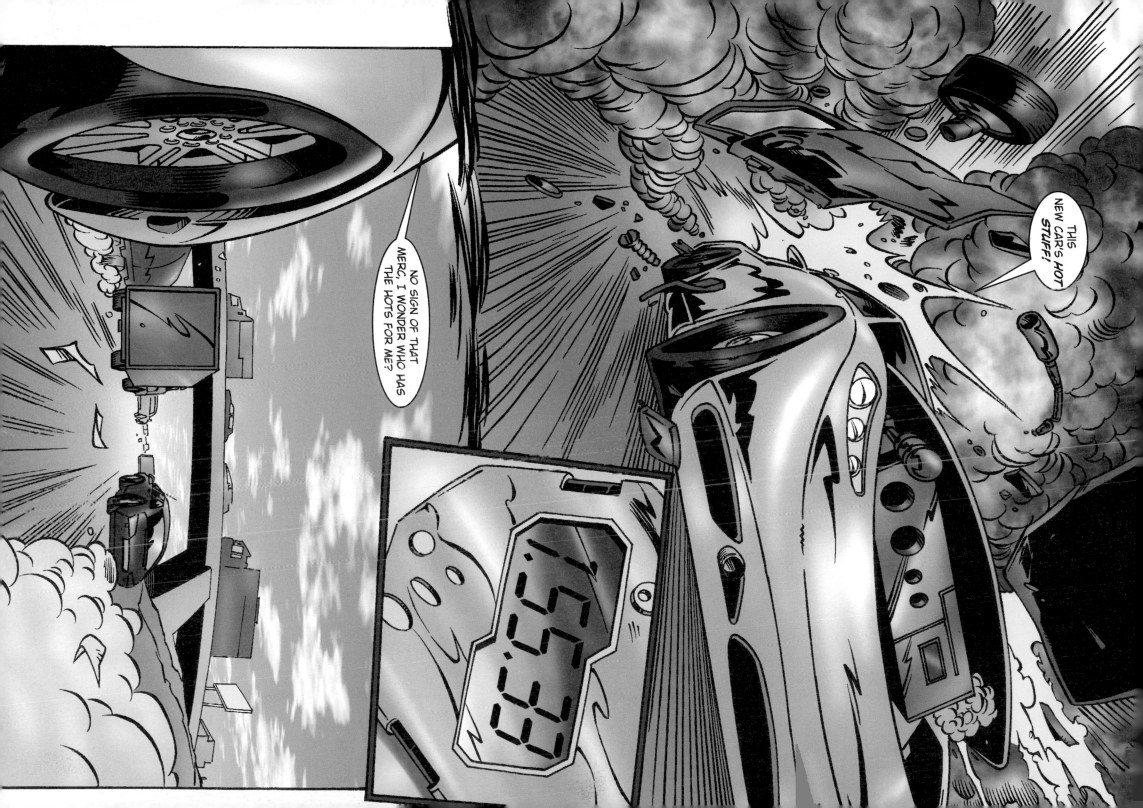

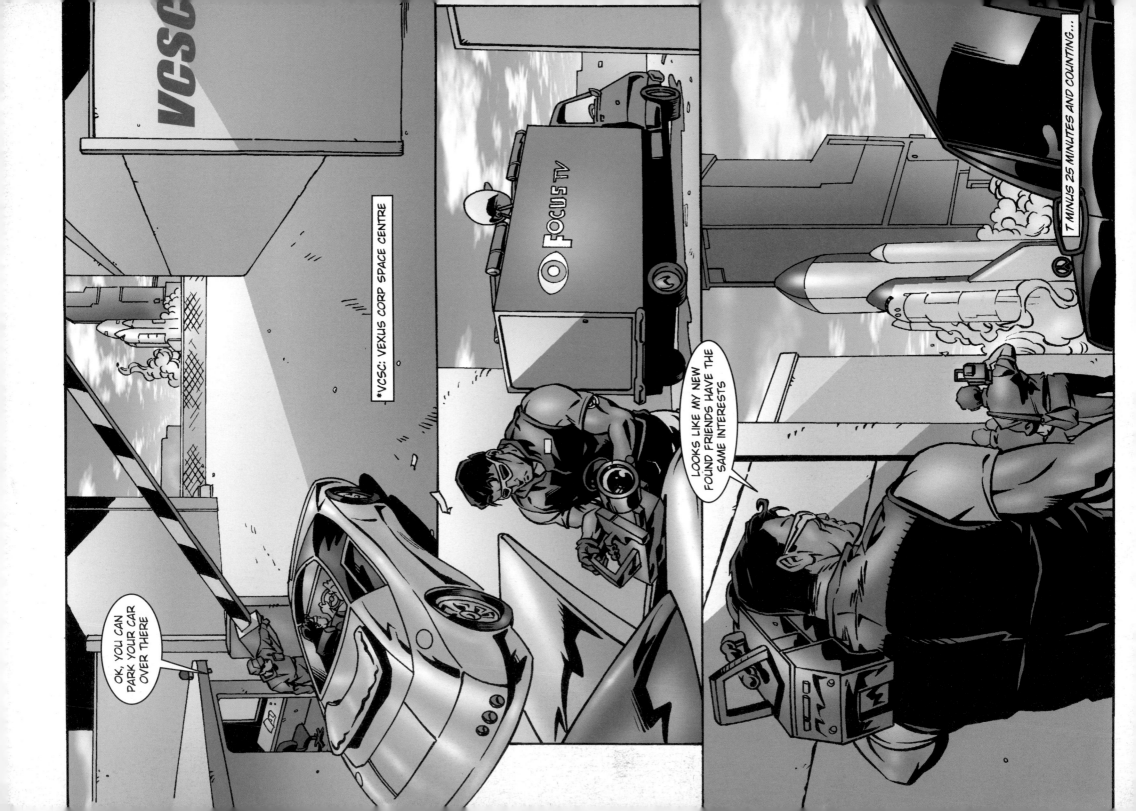

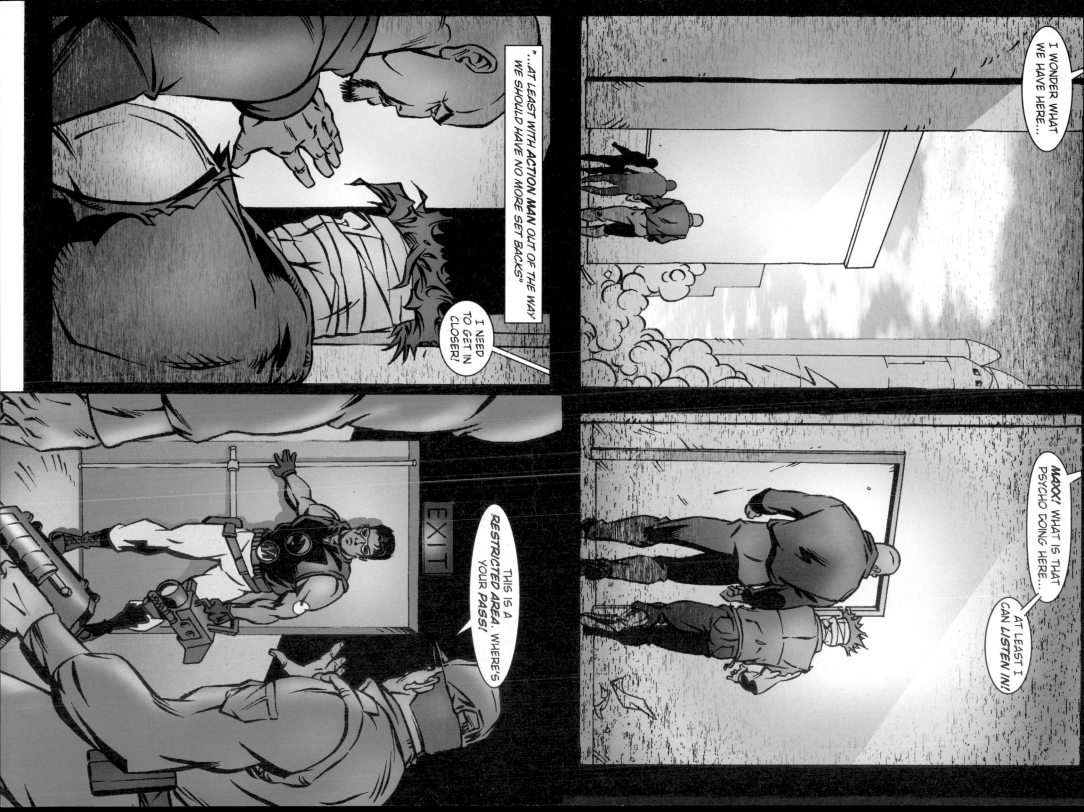

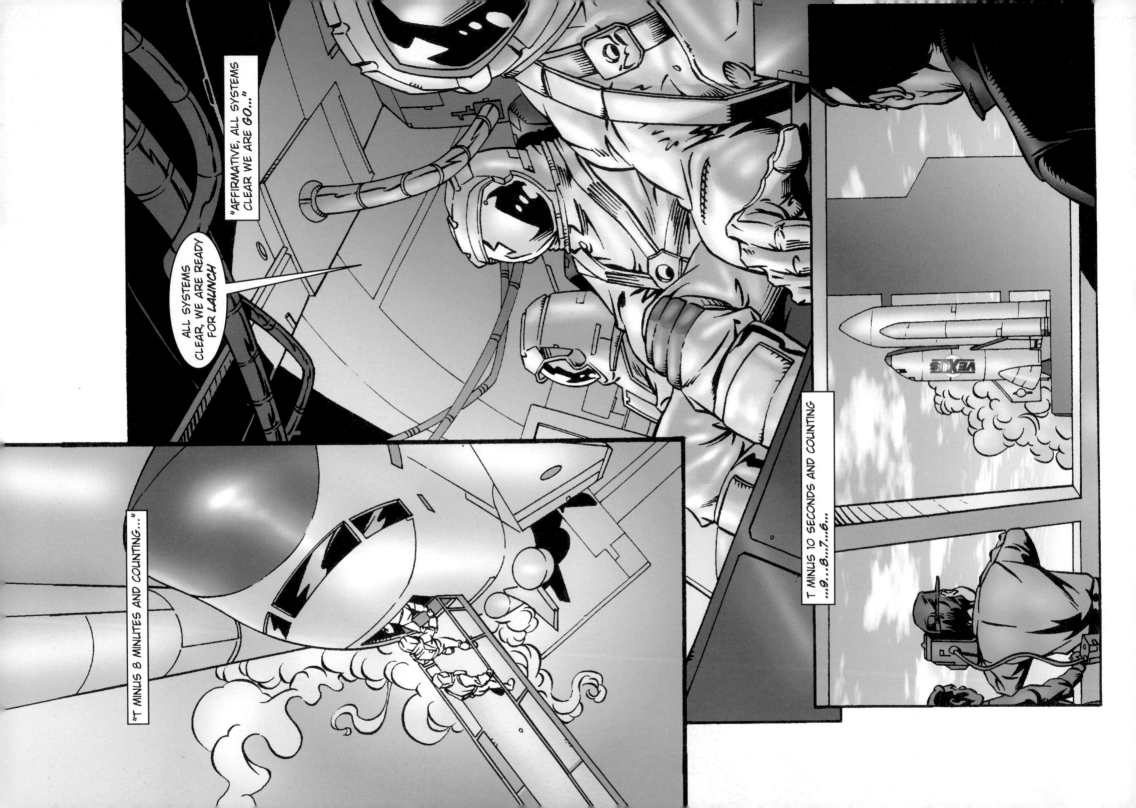

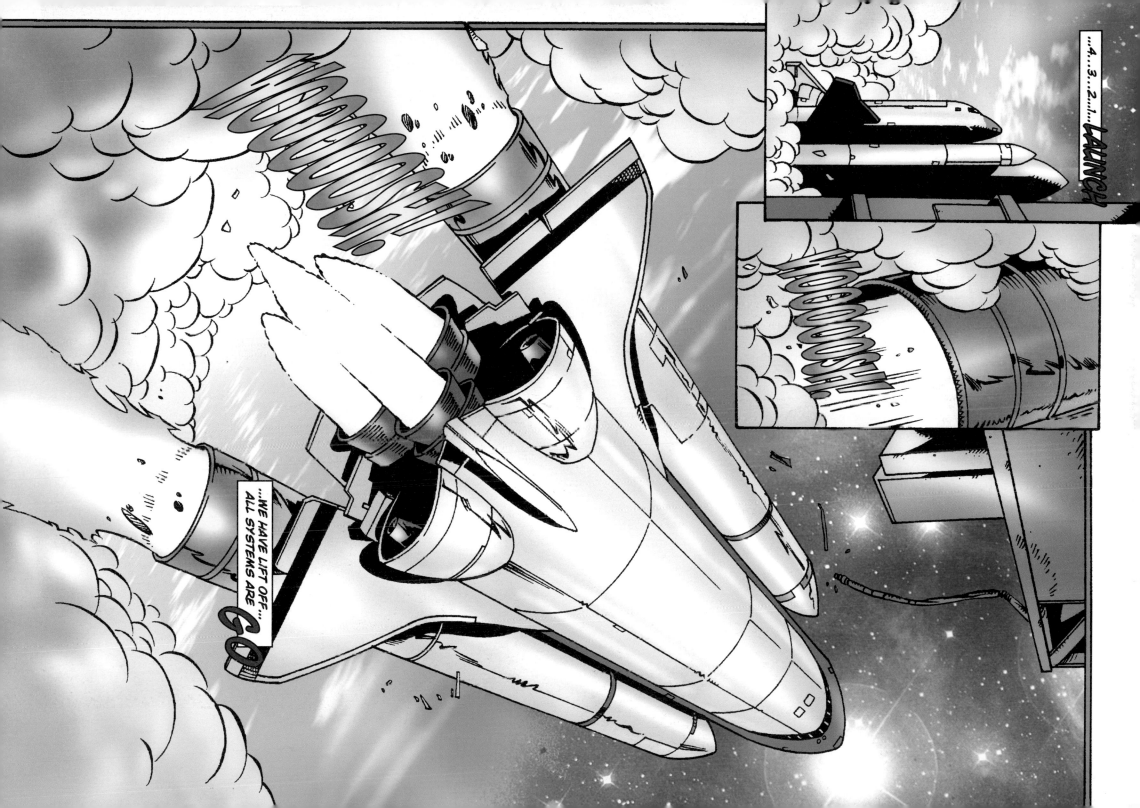

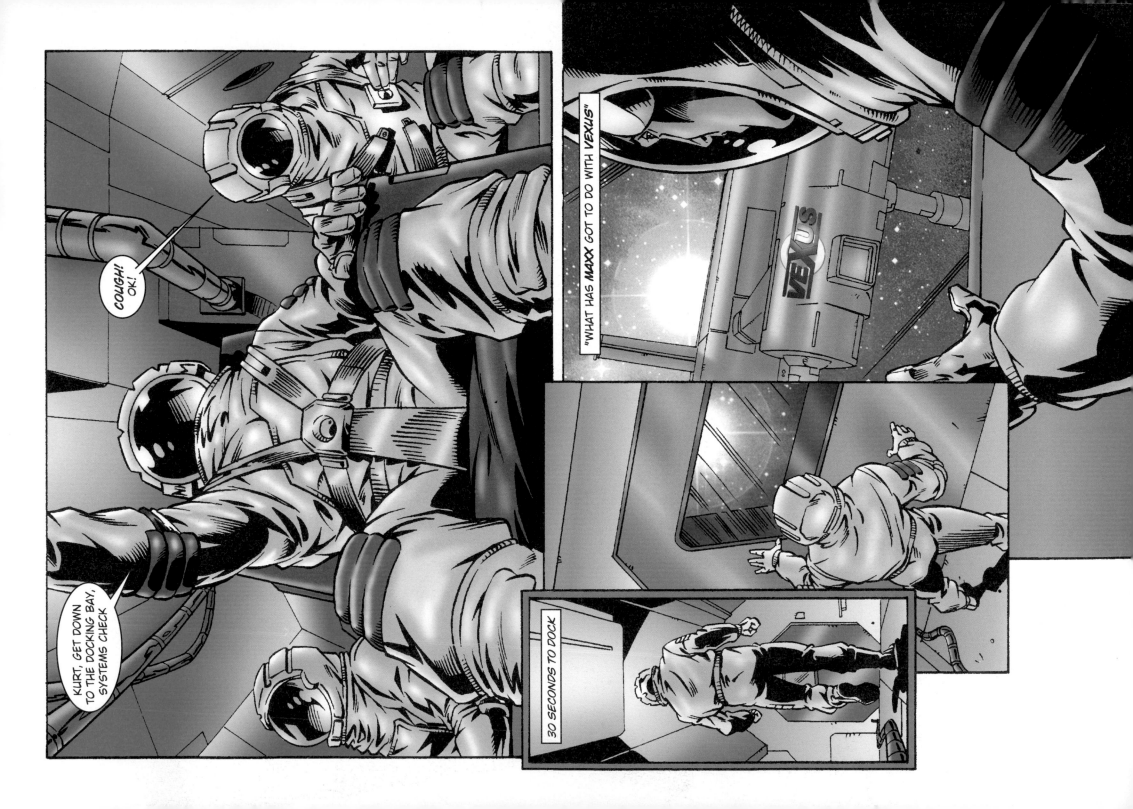

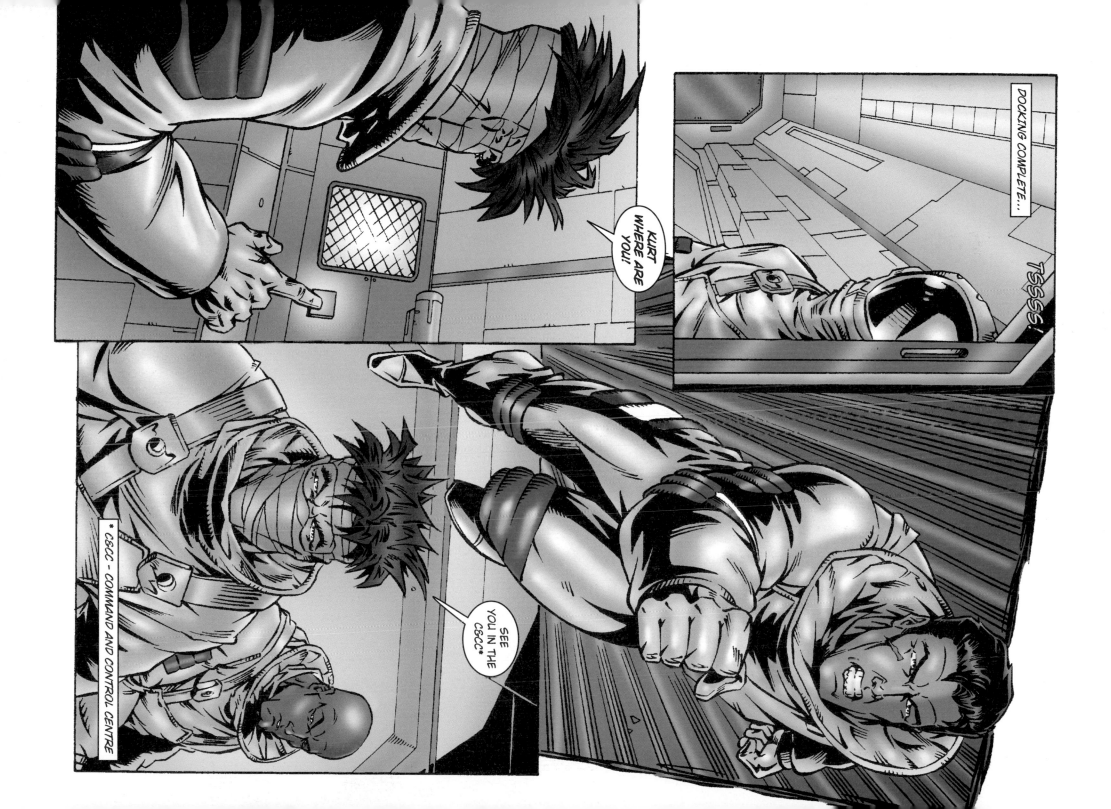

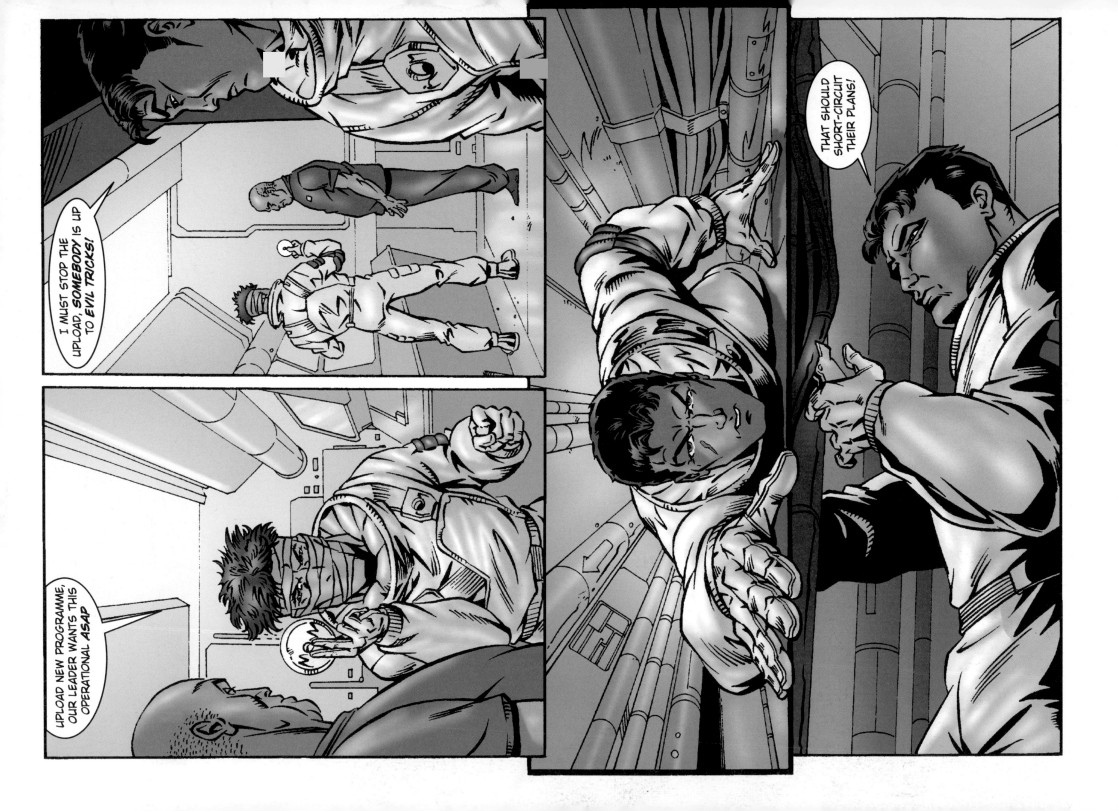

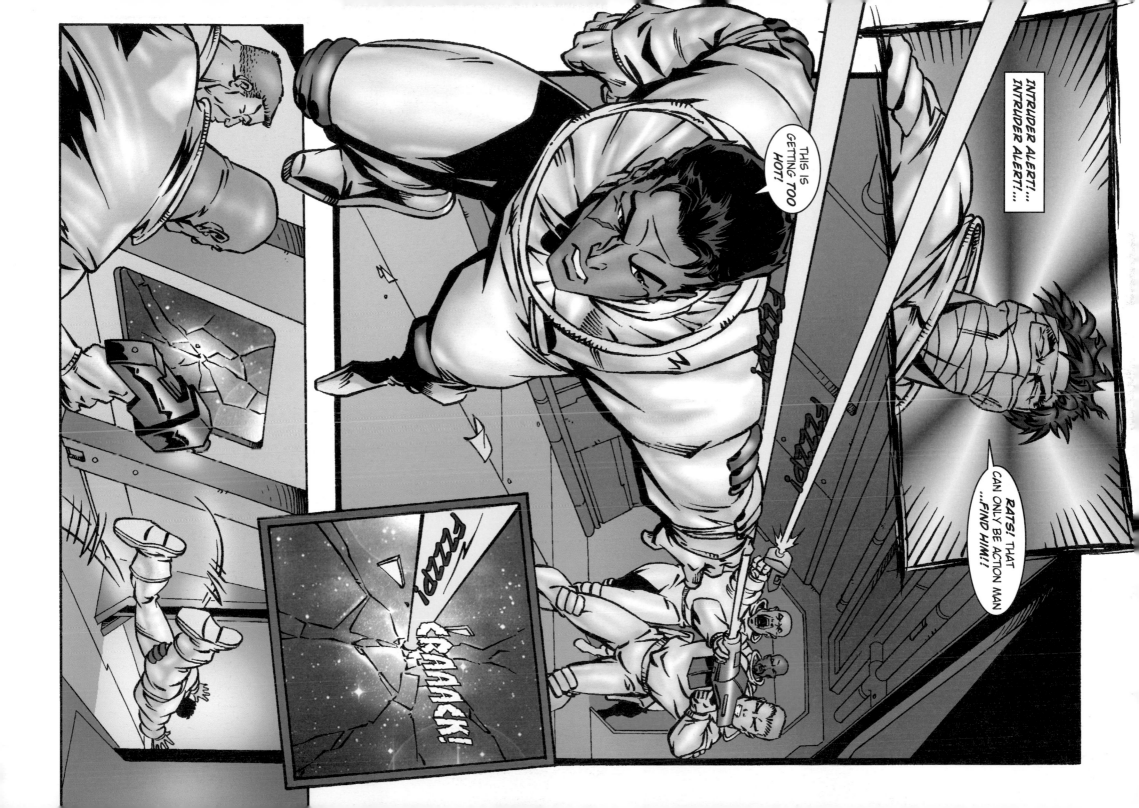

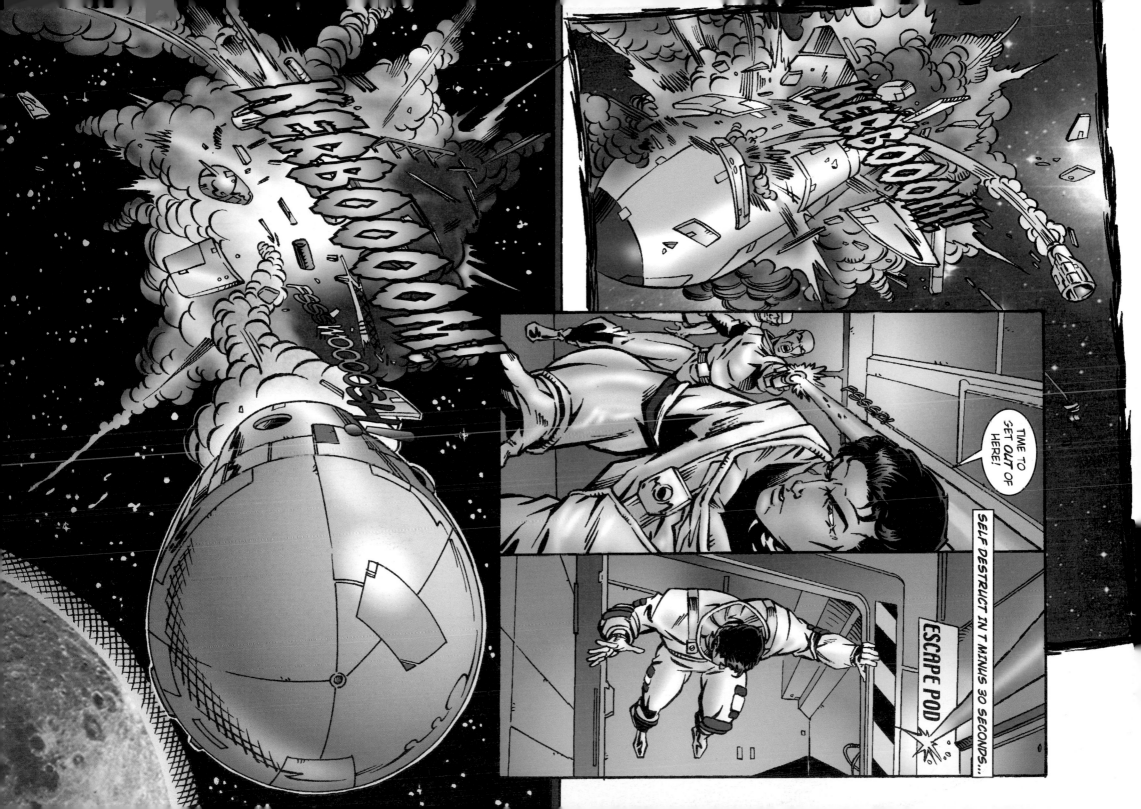

ACTION MAN

MaXXimum Velocity

Action Man needs to debrief the European Defence Agency.

Can you help him extract the key information from the mission he has just completed.

Answer the questions by ticking the correct solution.

29

1 . What first tries to stop Action Man?

A. Car crash
B. Traffic jam
C. Oil tanker

2 . What causes the accident?

A. Bad driving
B. Tyres explode
C. Ice on road

3 . Who may have been driving the mysterious black car?

A. Police
B. Government Agency
C. MaXX

4 . What is MaXX doing on the space station?

A. Changing the orbit
B. Downloading a new programme
C. Activating the station

5 . How does Action Man try to stop MaXX's plans?

A. By destroying the computer
B. By using a virus
C By cutting the network wires

6 . Who sets off the self destruct sequence?

A. MaXX
B. Action Man
C. Computer

7 . Which organisation is MaXX linked to?

A. CIA
B. VeXus Corp
C. Russian Mafia

Answers can be found on page 31

MIC

Colour in this drawing of Action Man 2000

ACTION MAN

Mission Zone QUICK ACCESS CARD

Equipment QUICK ACCESS CARD

Reconnaissance QUICK ACCESS CARD

Mission Debriefing

EDA Equipment Designer

File   Edit   Type   View   Window   Help

31

**Design a new piece of equipment for Action Man to use in space.
When you have done it paste it into this box.**

INITIATE   COMMS.   MISSION   STATUS   AM2000PDA

MIC

Missions Briefing: Paws for Thought

New Mail

INCOMING E-MAIL - SECURE LINK ENCODING

ubCChþg8 xic nhß lahEoaD umClomß lam mckiðm ðhl
khþdlþrbþo u155 aic Jmmg DßikdmJ ic niß iC i BmfÞm
fÞdÞlþg ßmobhþq bg umhßkh...oßþl zmimßmmkm iegal
MM.Q kiEcm8 qþbbie mfþlmgkm bþJbkiÞmC DaiD u155 bC
ChÞmahG ebgdml Dh 3m5EC...ubCCbhþg8 thkiÞm Dam mckiðm
Þhl igl DßikÞ lhGß u155...3mmßnl * keiÞnl ebgdC Dh
3m5EC...

...DECODING ENCRYPTION

Mission: Paws for Thought

Message:
The escape pod containing Maxx has been tracked as
far as a remote mountain region in Mexico...
Grid Reference Alpha 22.6

Cause:
Initial evidence indicates that Maxx is somehow
linked to Vexus...

Mission:
Locate the escape pod and track down Maxx...
Verify & clarify links to Vexus...

...end transmission

ACTION MAN

QUICK ACCESS CARD — Mission Zone

QUICK ACCESS CARD — Equipment

QUICK ACCESS CARD — Reconnaissance

ACTION MAN

EDA Geographic Reconnaissance Data

Location: Middle America, bordering the Caribbean Sea and the Gulf of Mexico, between Belize and the US and bordering the North Pacific Ocean, between Guatemala and the US

Geographic co-ordinates: 23 00 N, 102 00 W

Climate: varies from tropical to desert

Terrain: high, rugged mountains, low coastal plains, high plateaus, and desert

Elevation extremes: lowest point: Laguna Salada -10 m

highest point: Volcan Pico de Orizaba 5,700 m

Natural resources: petroleum, silver, copper, gold, lead, zinc, natural gas, timber

Population: 98,552,776 (July 1998 est.)

Languages: Spanish, various Mayan, Nahuatl, and other regional indigenous

Government type: federal republic operating under a centralized government

Mission 2 - Satellite Uplink

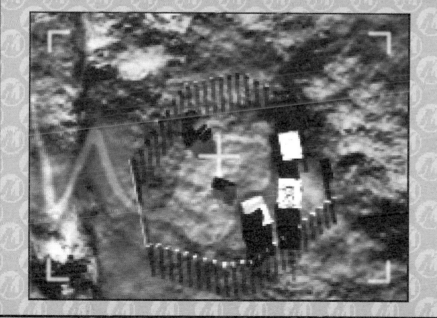

100% | Live Feed

Mexico - Population

Mexico - Temperature/Climate

Mexico - Flora & Fauna

33

MIC

ACTION MAN

Mission Zone
QUICK ACCESS CARD

Equipment
QUICK ACCESS CARD

Reconnaissance
QUICK ACCESS CARD

Mission Data : Equipment

Mountain Bike Xtreme

Working in the field on tough new assignments you have to choose the right equipment. You never know what might come in handy.

Select your equipment from the list below.

- Explosives
- Scuba Gear
- Binoculars
- Nija Weapons
- Canoe
- 4x4 Jeep
- Hanglider
- Mountain Bike
- PDA2000
- Tool Kit

Frame: Carbon fibre and magnesium composite with adjustable ceramic shock absorbers

EFT: Epoxy resin fluid filled all terrain tyres (stops all punctures and blowouts/ automatically changes pressure to counter different surface conditions)

AGS: 32 gear automatic gearing system, manual override handlebar grip

Weapons: 1x Multipurpose Sidewinder missiles Range 1km

Navigation: GPS (Global Positioning System)

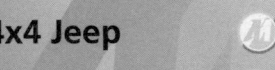

Briefed

Equipped

Accept Mission

Don't forget your helmet & knee pads

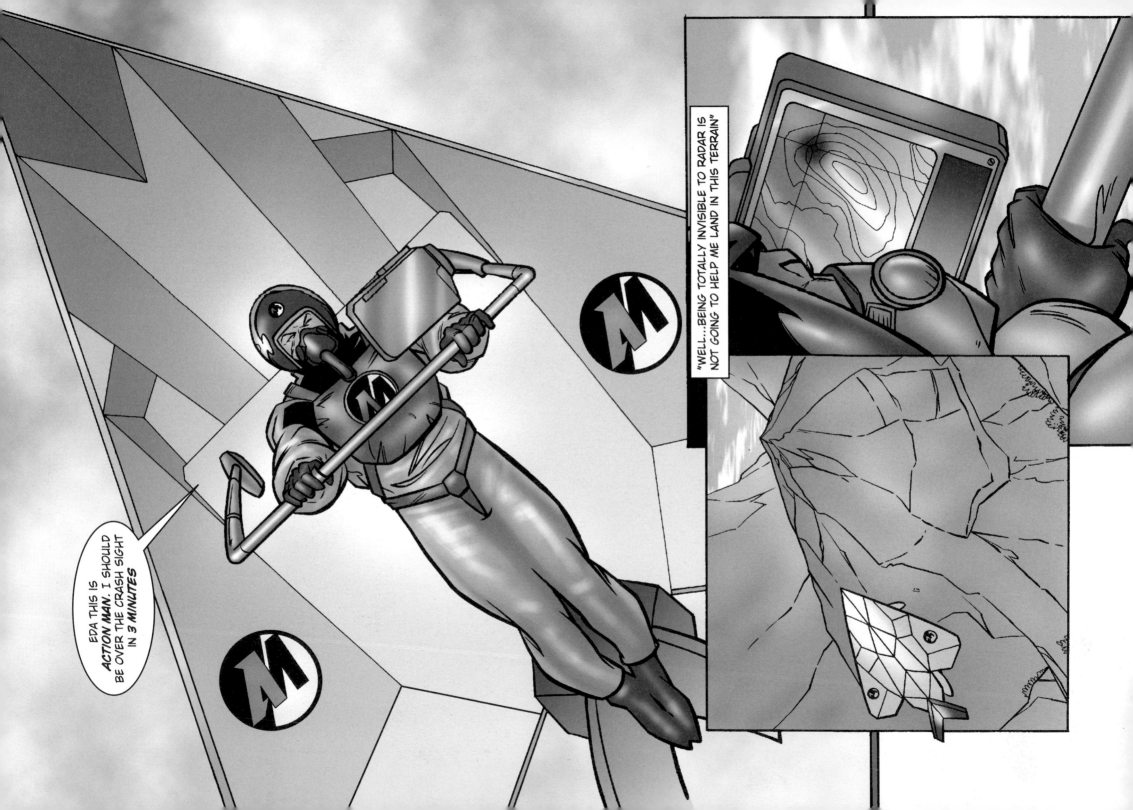

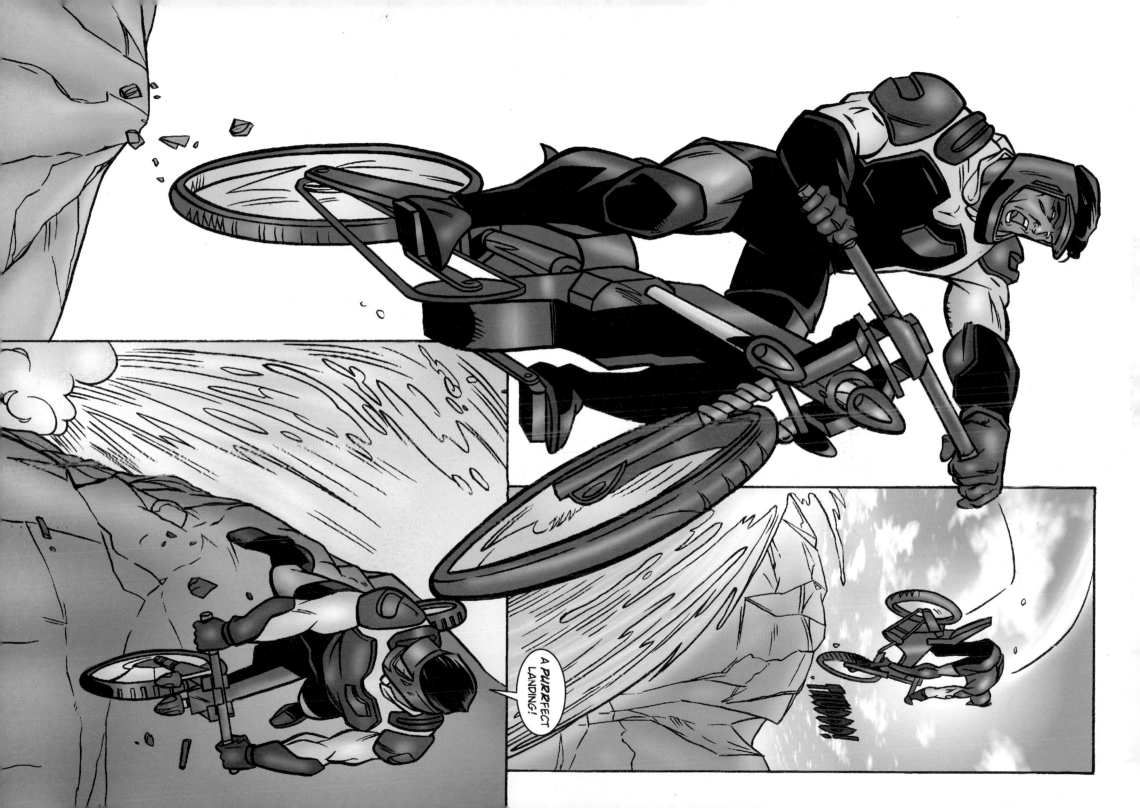

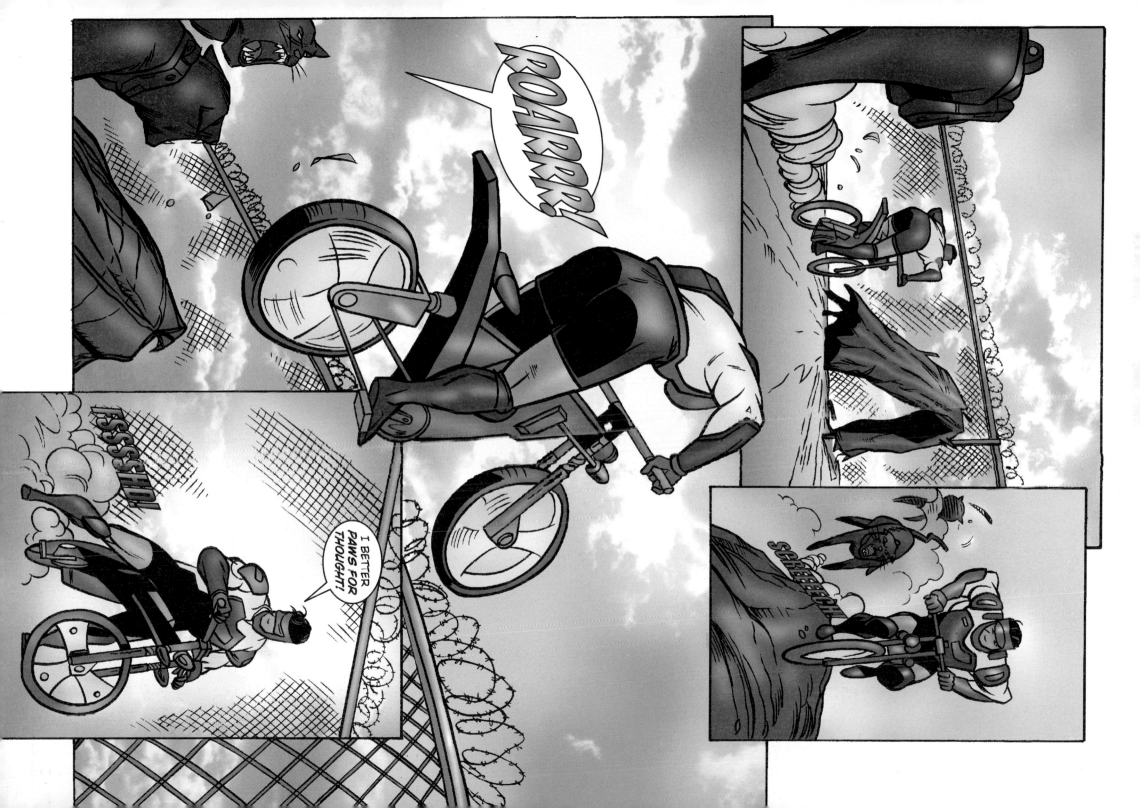

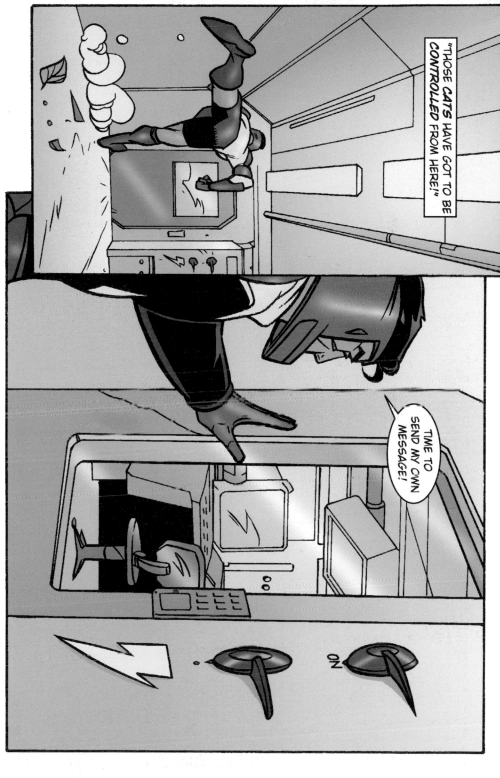

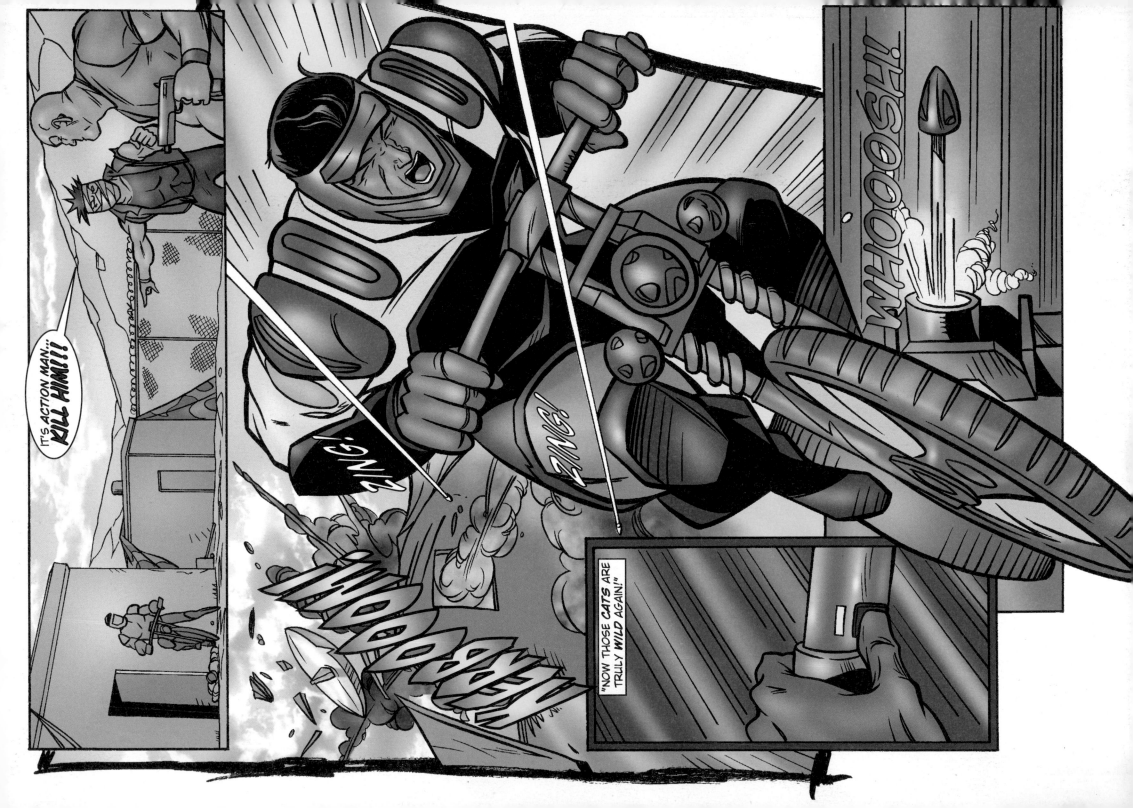

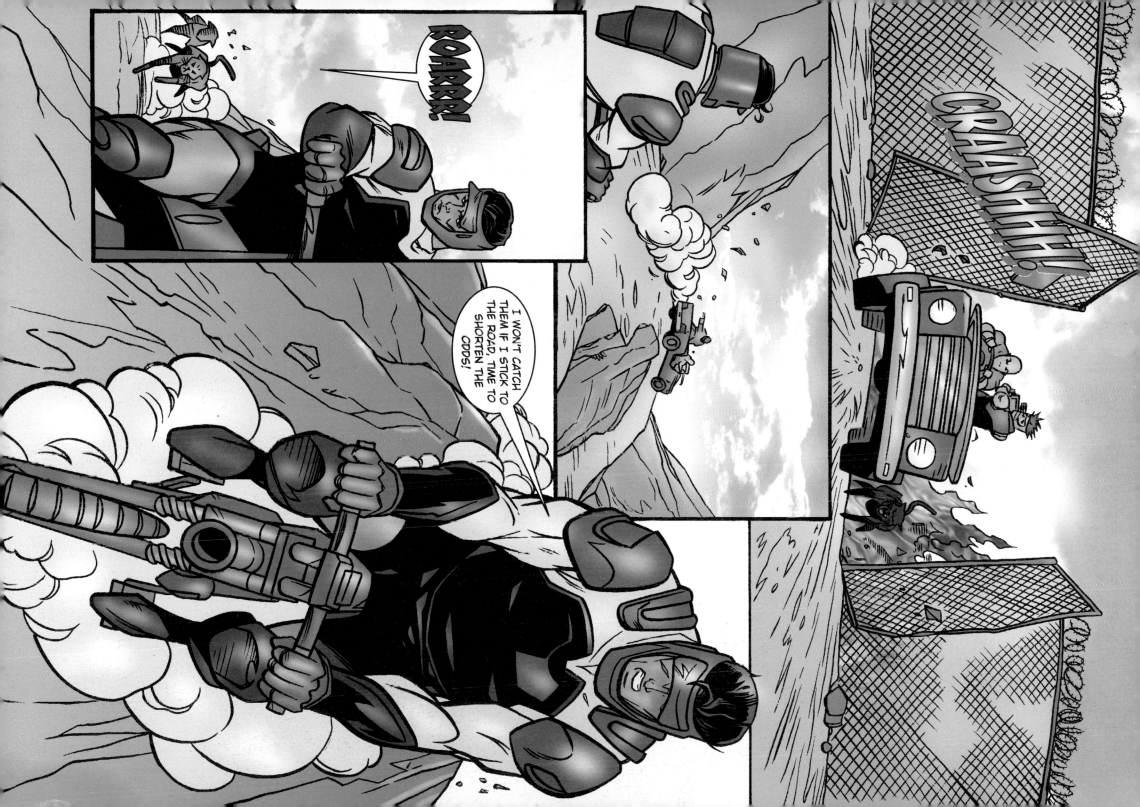

ACTION MAN

Mission Zone QUICK ACCESS CARD

Equipment QUICK ACCESS CARD

Reconnaissance QUICK ACCESS CARD

Mission Debriefing

Paws for Thought

Action Man needs to debrief the European Defence Agency.

Can you help him extract the key information from the mission he has just completed.

Answer the questions by ticking the correct solution.

54

1. What is on the panthers body?

A. Nothing

B. Electronic collar

C. Gold chain

2. Where does Action Man track MaXX to?

A. Deserted village

B. Secret VeXus camp

C. The city

3. What is the place for?

A. Army training camp

B. Village

C. Satellite control station

4. What are the collars on the animals for?

A. To control them

B. To identify them

C. To tie them up with

5. Where are the cats controlled from?

A. The main building

B. The space station

C. Another secret base

6. How does Action Man disable the control of the cats?

A. Sleeping gas

B. Destroys the main building

C. Switches of the power

7. What else could the VeXus Corp control if they can control cats?

A. Vehicles

B. Plants

C. People

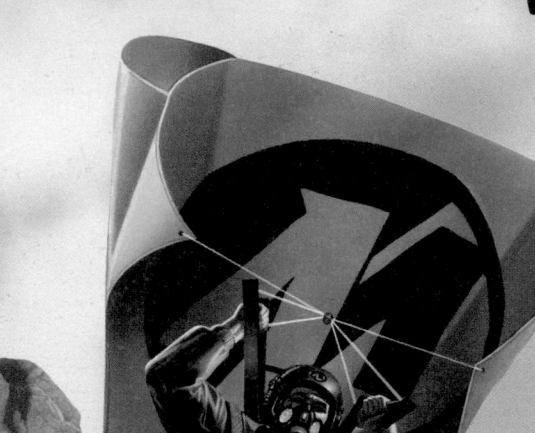

Answers can be found on page 56

Mission Debriefing

EDA Equipment Designer

File Edit Type View Window Help

Design a new piece of XTreme equipment for Action Man to use and when you have done it paste it into this box.

Answers from page 54:

1. What is on the panthers body?
B. Electronic collar

2. Where does Action Man track Maxx to?
B. Secret Vexus camp

3. What is the place for?
C. Satellite control station

4. What are the collars on the animals for?
A. To control them

5. Where are the cats controlled from?
A. The main building

6. How does Action Man disable the control of the cats?
B. Destroys the main building

7. What else could the Vexus Corp control if they can control cats?
C. People

QUICK ACCESS CARD — Mission Zone

QUICK ACCESS CARD — Equipment

QUICK ACCESS CARD — Reconnaissance

ACTION MAN

⊞ New Mail

INCOMING E-MAIL - SECURE LINK ENCODING

ubCCbhg8 vmDCki@m umCCiom8 3m5EC aiC i BmCmiBka nikbebDI
1mm@ bg Dam ifiJhg cEgoem CDElIbgo BiBm * mgligomBml
C@mkbmC... kiECm8 1am kiD C@mkbmC 1bCkhFmBml bg umHbkh
GmBm ghD bglbomghEC! Dh DaiD Bmobhg...DamI hBBobgiDm nBhf
0hEDa ifmBbki...ubCCbhg8 thkiDm * qgFmCDboiDm Dam zmCmi
Bka nikbebDI# i@@Bmamgl ui55...

...DECODING ENCRYPTION

Mission: Netscape
Message: VeXus has a research facility
deep in the Amazon jungle studying
rare & endangered species
Cause: The cat species discovered in
Mexico were not indigenous* to that
region...
...they originate from South America
Mission: Locate & Investigate the
Research Facility, apprehend MaXX.

*indigenous - belonging naturally to a place

...end transmission

EDA Secure Channel

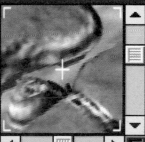

⊞ Satellite Up... ⬏

ACTION MAN

Mission Zone
QUICK ACCESS CARD

Equipment
QUICK ACCESS CARD

Reconnaissance
QUICK ACCESS CARD

Mission Data : Netscape

EDA Geographic Reconnaissance Data

The Amazon Rainforest covers about two million square miles of land in South America. It covers a vast portion of Brazil.

The Amazonian rainforest can be extremely dense in some areas and very sparse in others. In some areas vegetation is so thick that sunlight can't even reach the forest floor. There are over a million different species of animals including mammals, birds, insects, and spiders living in the Amazon.

The Amazon River is 4000 miles long and starts in the Andes, rushing through waterfalls and gorges before entering the enormous tropical Amazon Basin.

As it's name suggests the rainforests have a very wet climate, and due to the proximity to the equator temperatures are quite high. This results in an uncomfortably humid climate.

The indigenous Indian population follows a primitive life style of farming, hunting and fishing, and the gathering of various forest products.

Heavy Industry such as mining, oil drilling and lumbering has caused an increase in the non-native population due to their need for a large workforce.

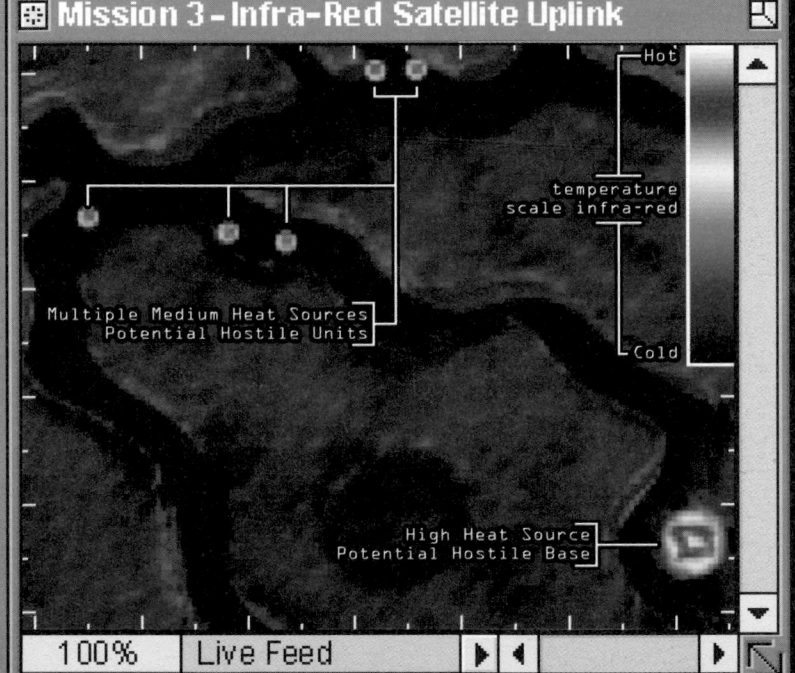

Mission 3 - Infra-Red Satellite Uplink

temperature scale infra-red

Hot

Cold

Multiple Medium Heat Sources
Potential Hostile Units

High Heat Source
Potential Hostile Base

100% Live Feed

Amazon Rainforest
Epselon 37.9

Mission Location

Hovercraft

Working in the field on tough new assignments you have to choose the right equipment. You never know what might come in handy.

Select your equipment from the list below.

- Canoe
- Scuba kit
- Drill
- Explosives
- Hovercraft
- Machete
- Binoculars
- PDA2000
- Net catcher
- Solar Speeder

Engine: water cooled 80hp

Thrust: 2x 10"/25.4cm prop. blades

Top speed water/ice: 65/95mph

Skirt: Multi-partitioned kevlar/ carbon thread fabric

Hover clearance: 12"/30.48cm

Climb gradient: 60%/1 in 6

Weapons: 2x Multipurpose fan missiles

1x 16mm machine gun

Search light: low light/infra-red

Navigation: GPS (Global Positioning System)

Briefed

Equipped

Accept Mission

You'll be blown away by this one!

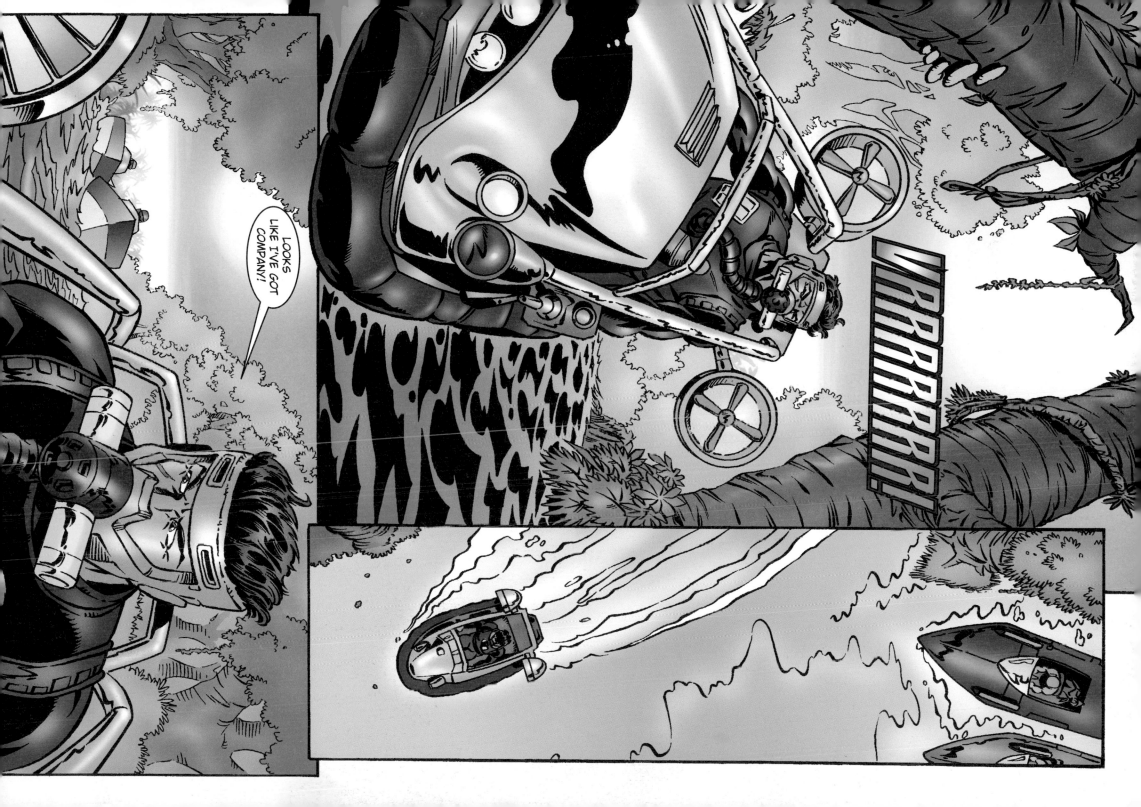

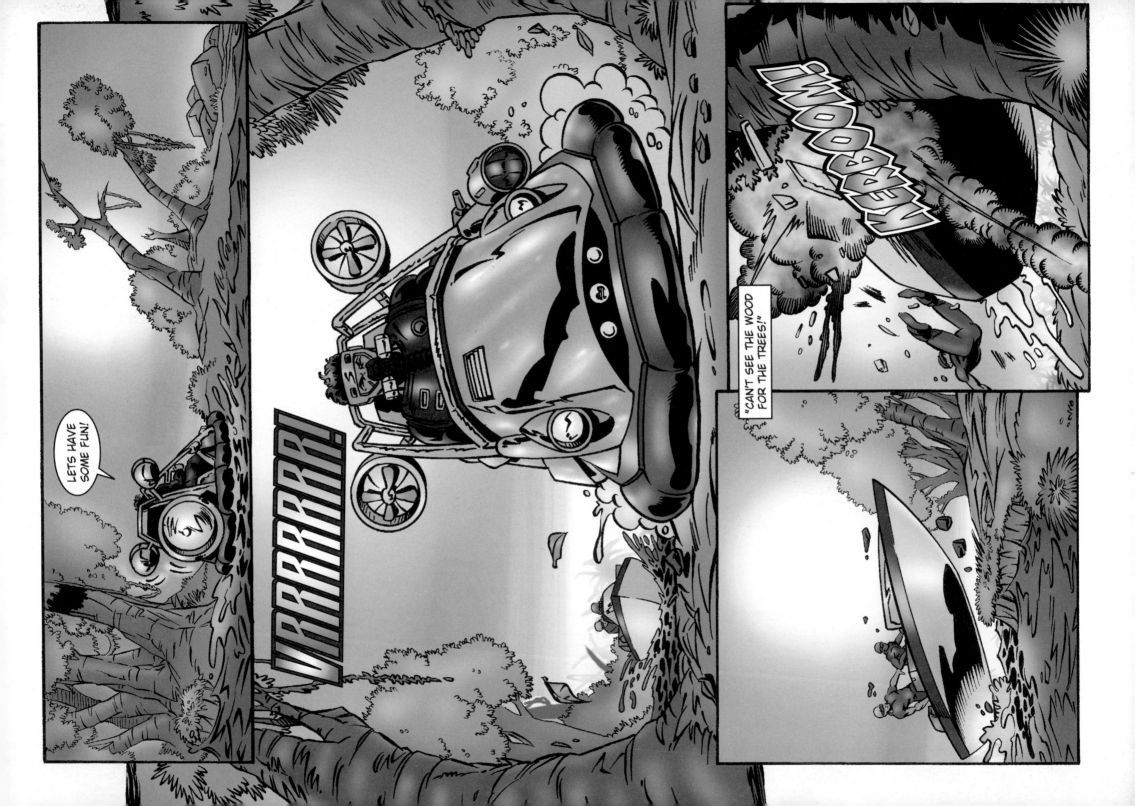

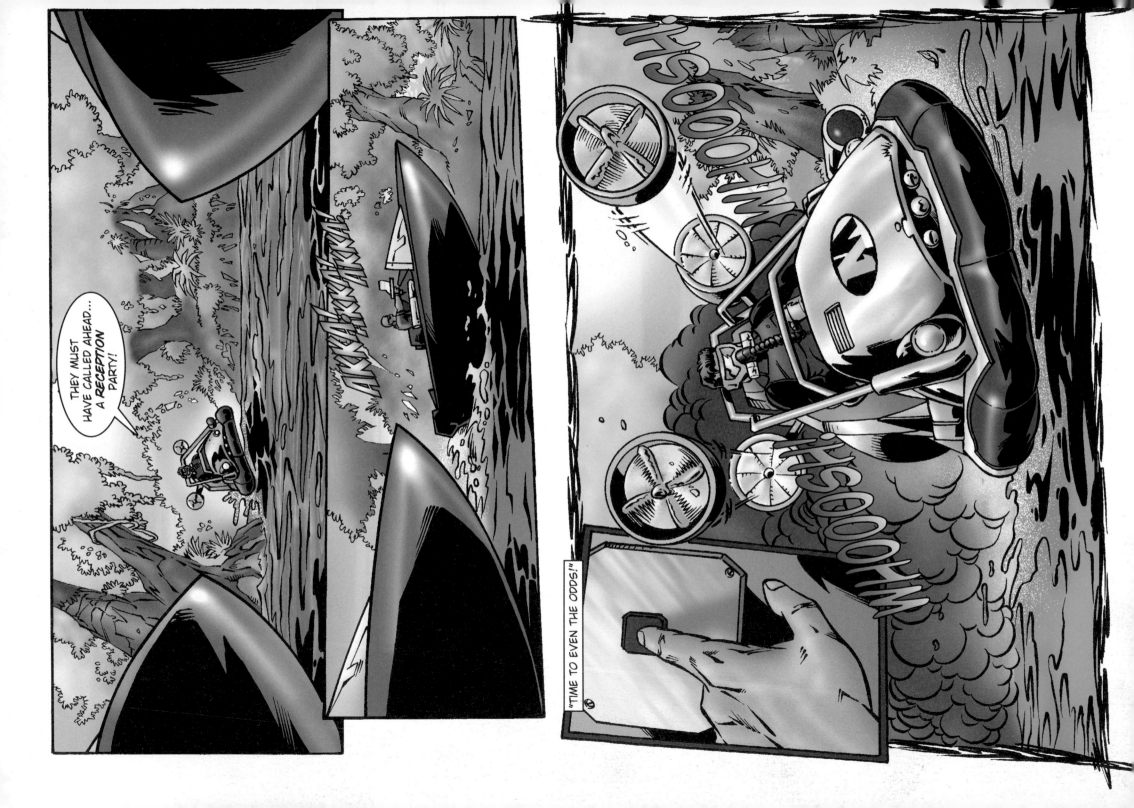

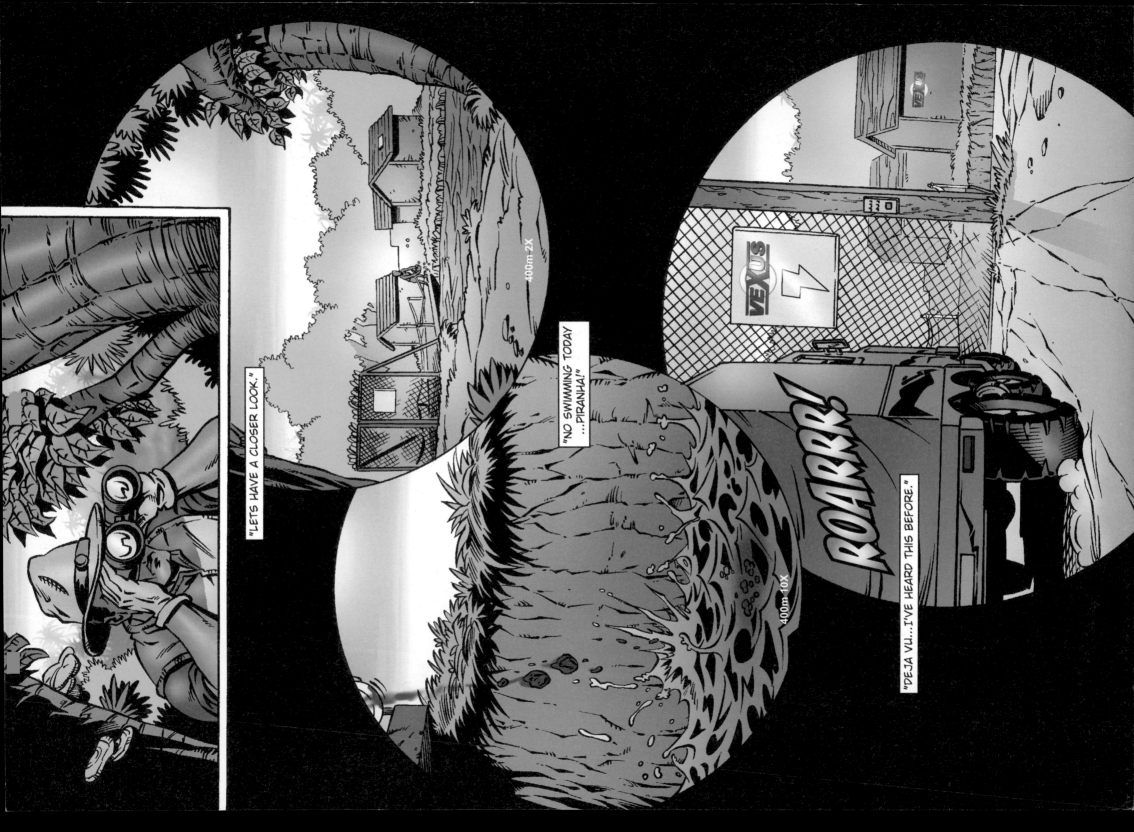

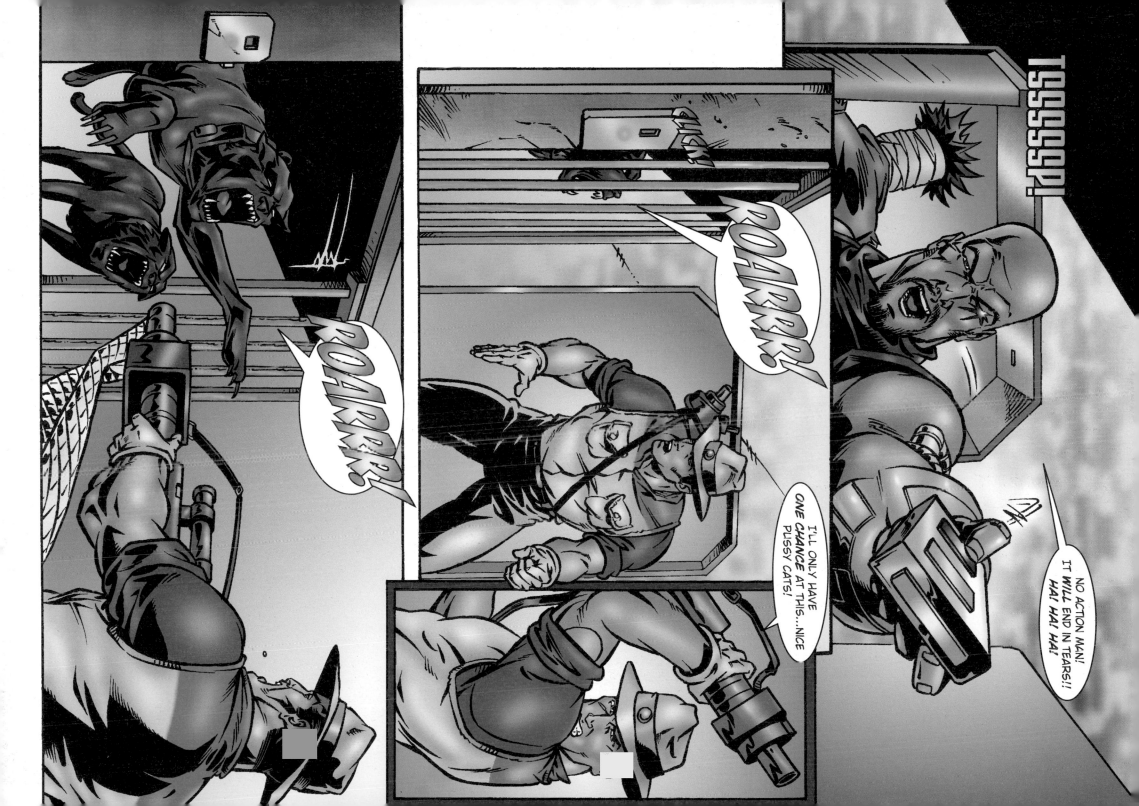

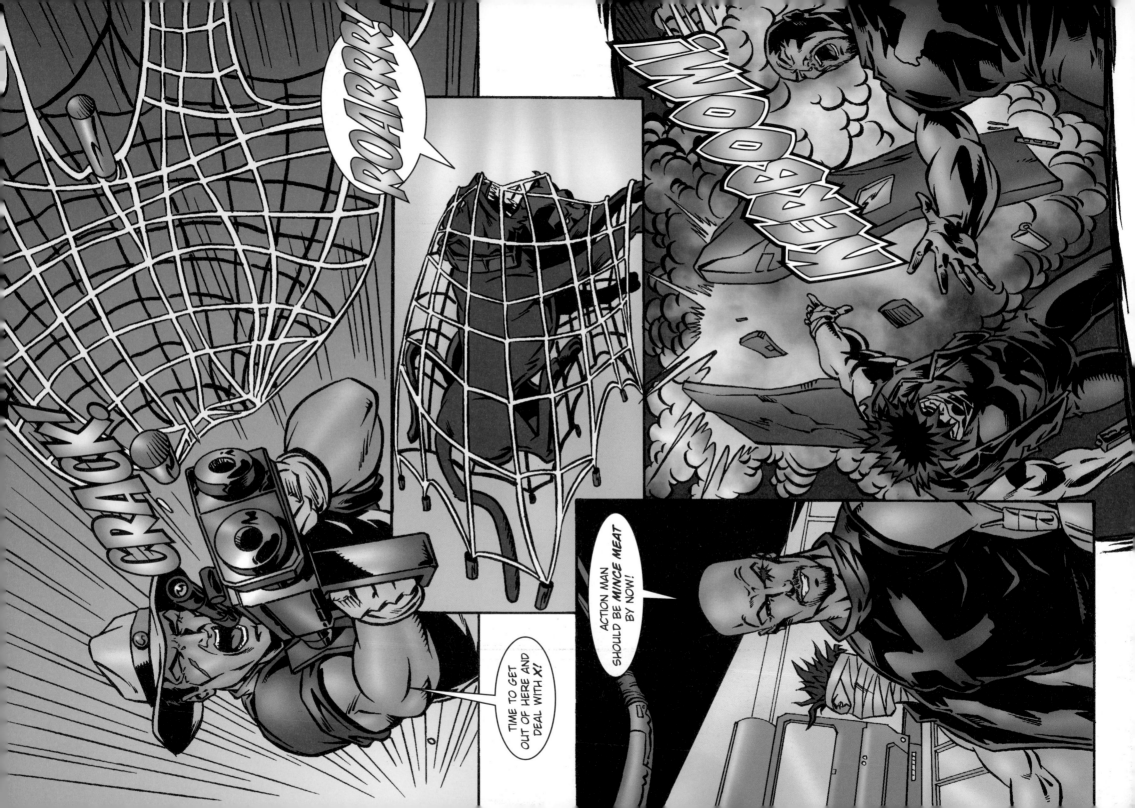

ACTION MAN

Mission Debriefing

Netscape

Action Man needs to debrief the European Defence Agency.

Can you help him extract the key information from the mission he has just completed.

Answer the questions by ticking the correct solution.

1 . Who owns the speed boats?

A.   VeXus Corp

B.   Government

C.   Russian Mafia

2 . Why can't Action Man swim to the camp?

A.   The waters too deep

B.   Piranha infested waters

C.   Leaches in the water

3 . How does Action Man get into the camp?

A.   In the back of a truck

B.   By parachute

C.   He tunnels his way in

4 . What are the crates in the lorry carrying?

A.   Weapons

B.   Computer chips

C.   Food rations

5 . Who is behind VeXus?

A.   Russian Mafia

B.   Dr. X

C   MaXX

6 . What is he planning?

A.   To control computers worldwide

B.   To destroy the arctic pole

C.   To rob Fort Knox

7 . How does Action Man capture MaXX?

A.   Stun gas

B.   Cats catch him

C.   Net gun

Answers can be found on page 81

INITIATE   COMMS.   MISSION   STATUS   *AM2000PDA*

MIC

Colour in this drawing of Action Man in the Jungle

ACTION MAN

Mission Zone
QUICK ACCESS CARD

Equipment
QUICK ACCESS CARD

Reconnaissance
QUICK ACCESS CARD

80

Mission Debriefing

EDA Equipment Designer

File   Edit   Type   View   Window   Help

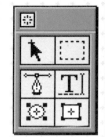

Answers from page 79:

1. Who owns the speed boats?

   A. VeXus Corp

2. Why can't Action Man swim to the camp?

   B. Piranha infested waters

3. How does Action Man get into the camp?

   A. In the back of a truck

4. What are the crates in the lorry carrying?

   B. Computer chips

5. Who is behind VeXus?

   B. Dr.X

6. What is he planning?

   A. To control computers worldwide

7. How does Action Man capture MaXX?

   C. Net Gun

81

Design a new piece of equipment for Action Man to use in the Jungle. When you have done it paste it into this box.

INCOMING E-MAIL - SECURE LINK ENCODING

ubCCbhg8 umoiJbPm@o@oumCCiom8 i eibom gEfImB hn BmEhBDC hn fDcCbgo @eigmC iqI jhiDc bg Dam iBmi dghGg ic Dam jmEfiI iBQibgoem iBm CBBnikbgo $ Daamm aic jmmg gh ikDPPbbt ebdm DabC Cbgkm eiCD kmgDEBI bg Dam LTRK+C. i eiBom BgimGbmI Biibcbbphg CbBBki aic Jmmg imbCbmI bg i 8mmPBbhCe! iBBfifp BgimBGimB Fhekigh...kiECm8 iB 5 GhEeI gmmmI i FmBI eiBom khiEBDmB iqI jicm Dh kbqBBhe iqI khShibgbqIm abc ikDBPbbbmC.. 4m jmemBPm DaiD oBPmg Dam BibbiDbhg emPmec iqI Dam fBCCbgo BmebBDC DaiD bc DaiD obPmg Dam 5+c gmG jiCm...ubCCbhg8 thkiDm 5+c jiCm * gmmBDiebCm jmmbBm MKKK imiiJepm...xBhkmmI GbDa 5DBmfm kiEDbhg8

...DECODING ENCRYPTION

Mission: Megabite

Message: A large number of reports of missing planes and boats in the area known as the Bermuda Triangle are surfacing - there has been no activity like this since last century in the 1970's. A large undersea radiation source has been detected in a previously dormant underwater volcano...

Cause: Dr X would need a very large computer and base to control and co-ordinate his activities.. We believe that given the radiation levels and the missing reports that this is most likely to be Dr X's new base...

Mission: Locate X's Base & neutralise before 2000 deadline...

...Proceed with Xtreme caution!

...end transmission

New Mail

Missions Briefing: Megabite

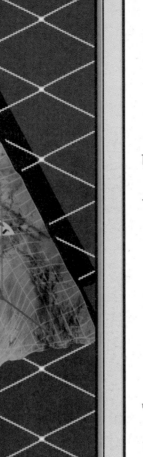

ACTION MAN

Mission Zone — QUICK ACCESS CARD

Equipment — QUICK ACCESS CARD

Reconnaissance — QUICK ACCESS CARD

EDA Geographic Reconnaissance Data

Volcanoes are mountains or hills that form due to build up of materials erupted through openings in the earth's surface. These openings are called volcanic vents.

Volcanoes are formed by the accumulation of magma. Magma is the molten rock that flows from below the earth's surface. When tiny droplets of magma are formed they begin to rise because the magma is lighter than the solid rock surrounding it. It usually does not go directly to the surface, but instead builds up in storage areas, called magma reservoirs, before it rises up volcanic vents and erupts onto the surface. After every eruption the magma dries and forms a new layer on the volcano.

Bermuda Triangle

Mission Location

The Bermuda Triangle is known as many things: The limbo of the lost, Twilight Zone and the Devil's Triangle just to name a few. The Bermuda Triangle is the area between Bermuda, Miami (Florida) and San Juan (Puerto Rico). It is a huge three-sided segment of the Atlantic Ocean bordered by Bermuda and hence the name the Bermuda Triangle.

There have been reports that in this area hundreds of ships and thousands of men have been disappearing for over 400 years. The most popular stories are: Christopher Columbus and the Devil's Triangle, "The Marie Celeste", Flight 19 and the disappearance of a DC-3 plane.

Mission 4 – CGI Enhanced Sonar

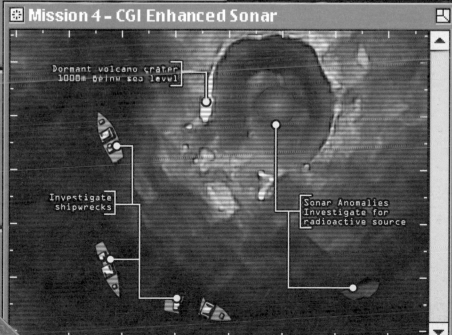

Dormant volcano crater 1000m below sea level

Investigate shipwrecks

Sonar Anomalies Investigate for radioactive source

100% | Live Feed

Volcanoes/The myth of the Bermuda Triangle

MIC

83

ACTION MAN

Mission Zone	Equipment	Reconnaissance	
QUICK ACCESS CARD	QUICK ACCESS CARD	QUICK ACCESS CARD	

Mission Data : Equipment

Ocean Mission DSV (Deep Sea Vehicle)

Working in the field on tough new assignments you have to choose the right equipment. You never know what might come in handy.

Select your equipment from the list below.

- DSV
- Scuba Kit
- Super Bike
- PDA2000
- Video Camera
- Drill
- Paraglyder
- Stealth Jet
- Canoe
- Explosives

Hull: Tungsten composite body with 5mm plexiglass screen

Maximum depth: 1.5km

Top speed: 36 knots

Propulsion: 2x rear mounted directional fans

Weapons: 1x Multipurpose torpedoes

Sensors: Sonar/low light 2000watt spot lights

Manipulator arm: Feather touch to one ton grip, integrated sample analyser

Navigation: Depth queued GPS (Global Positioning System)

Briefed

Equipped

Accept Mission

You'll be in deep water if you don't make the deadline

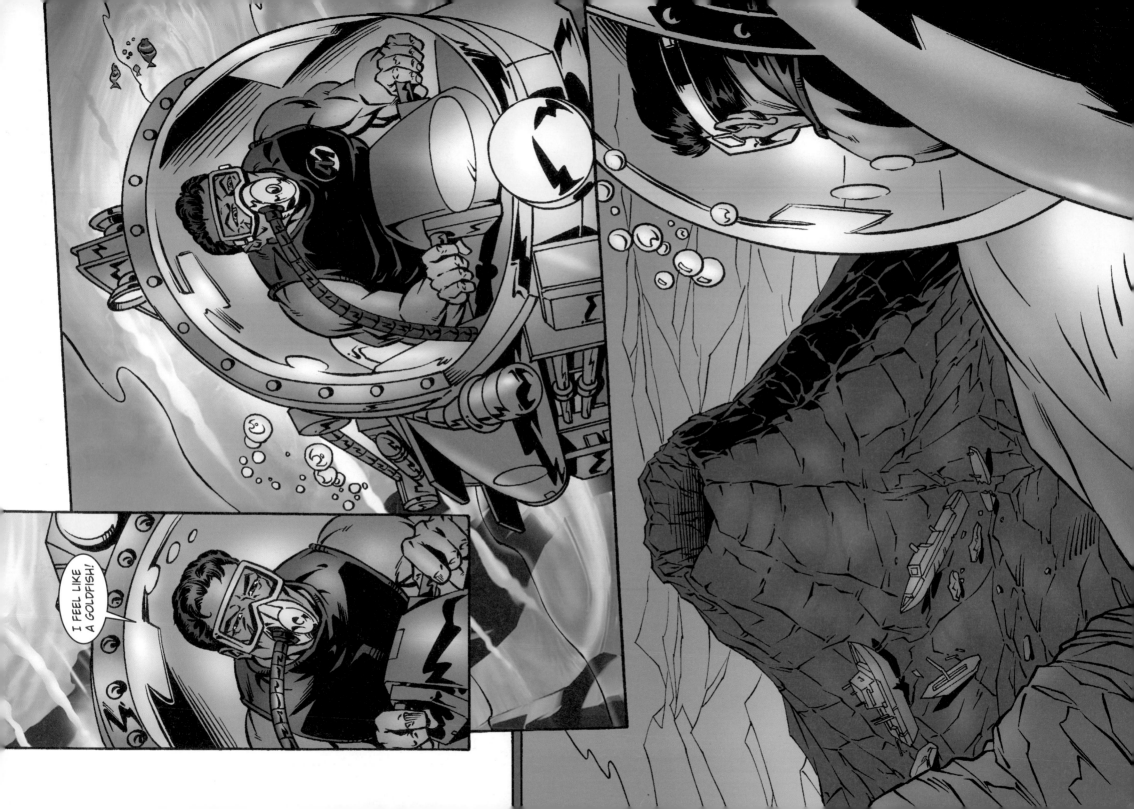

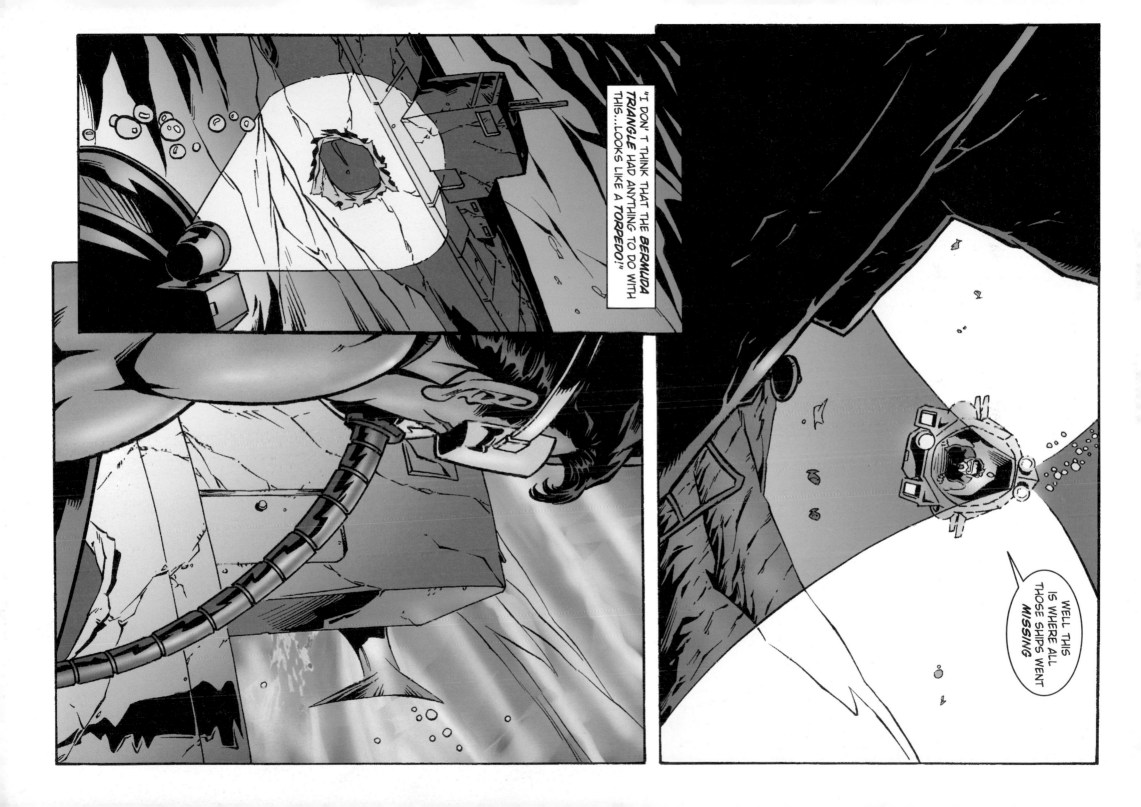

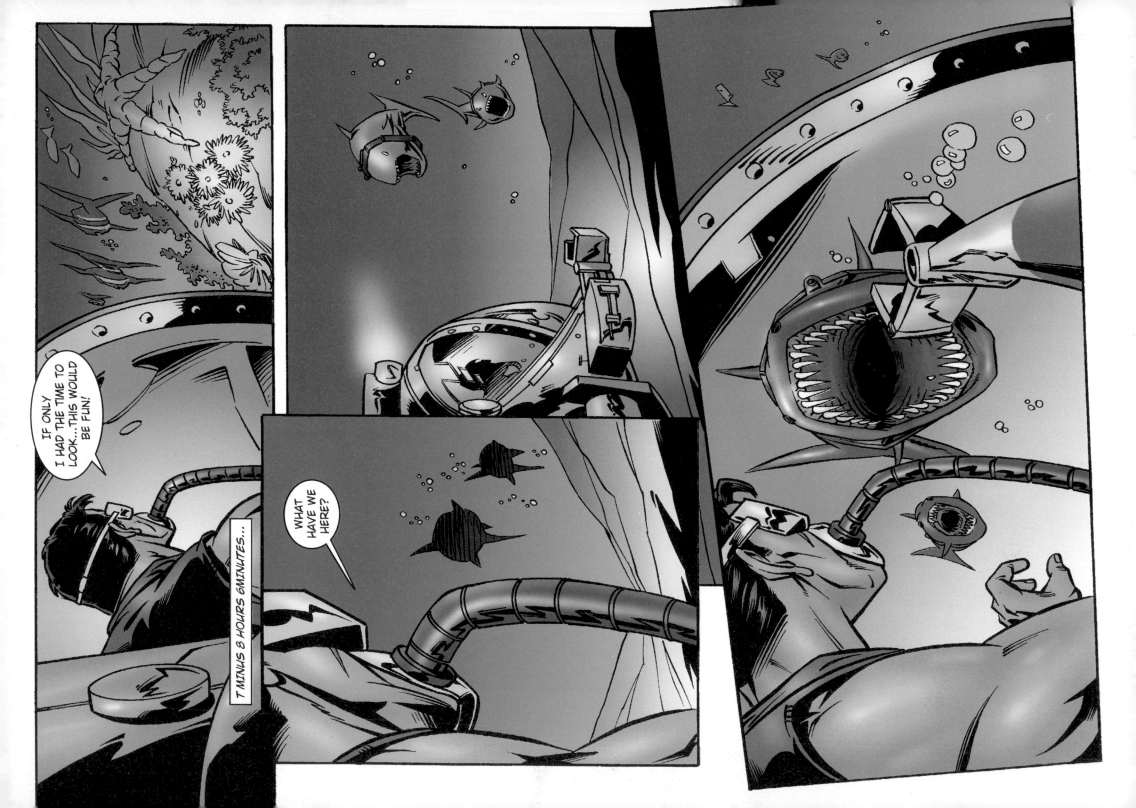

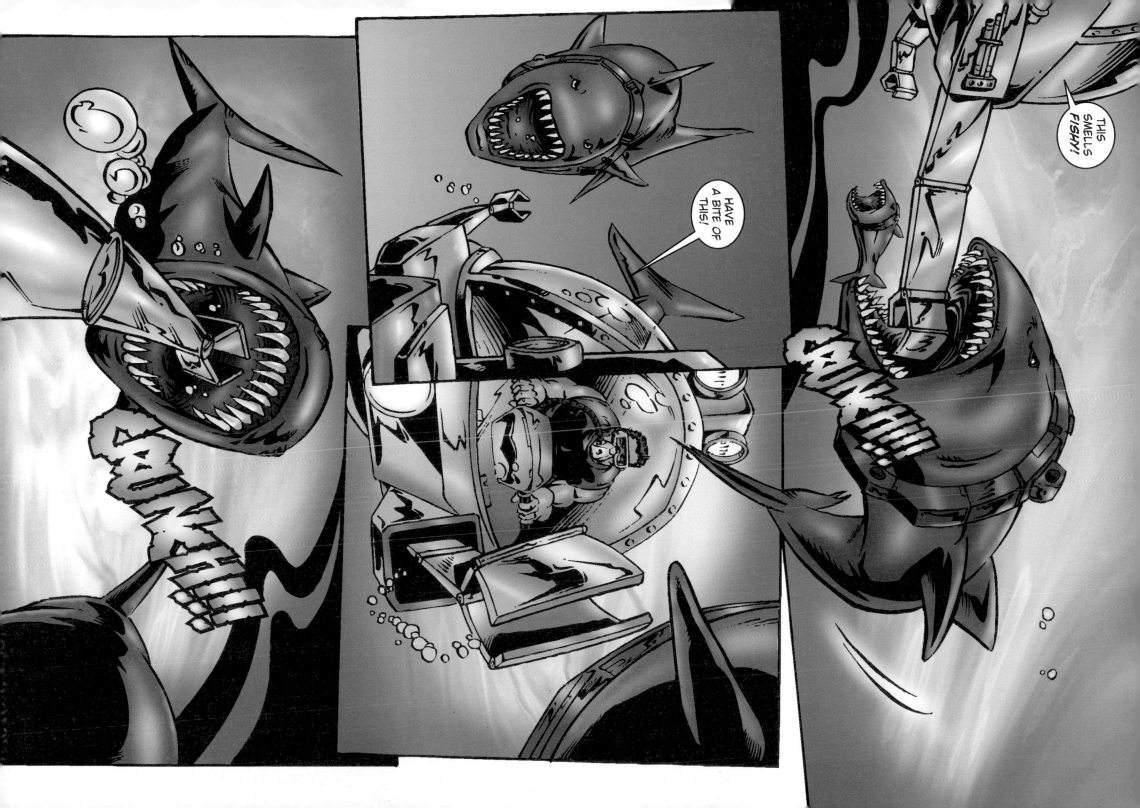

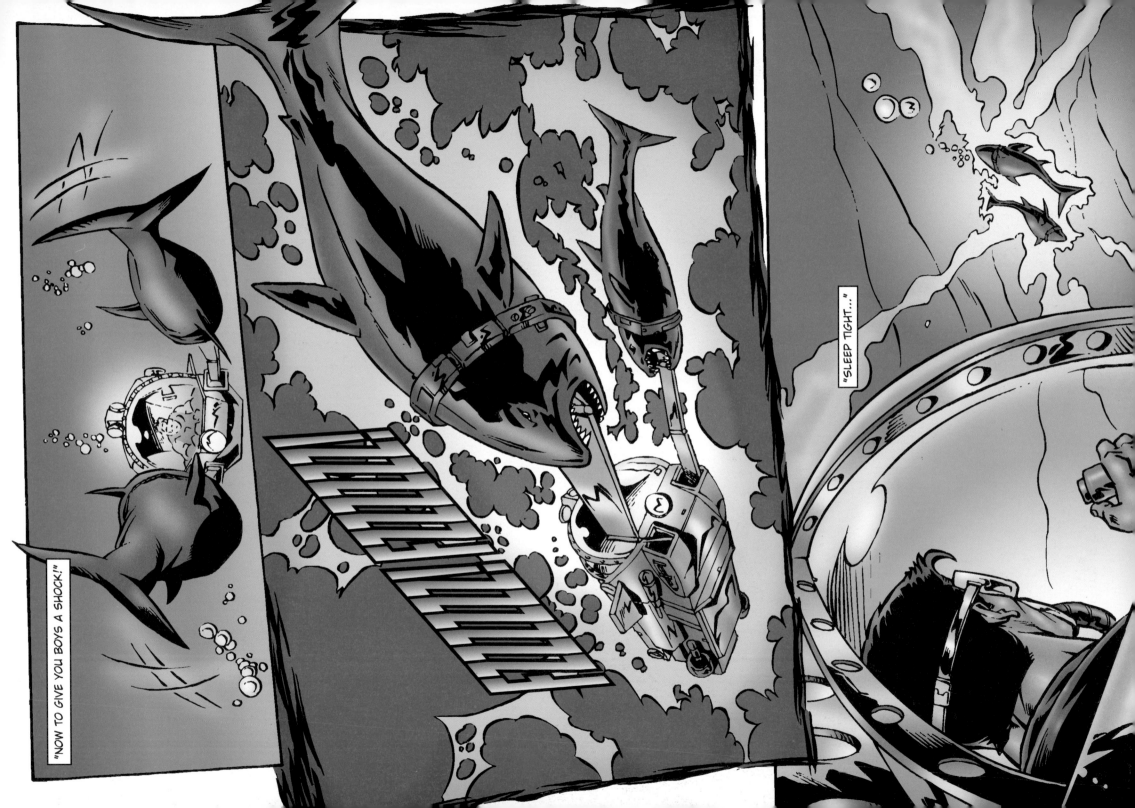

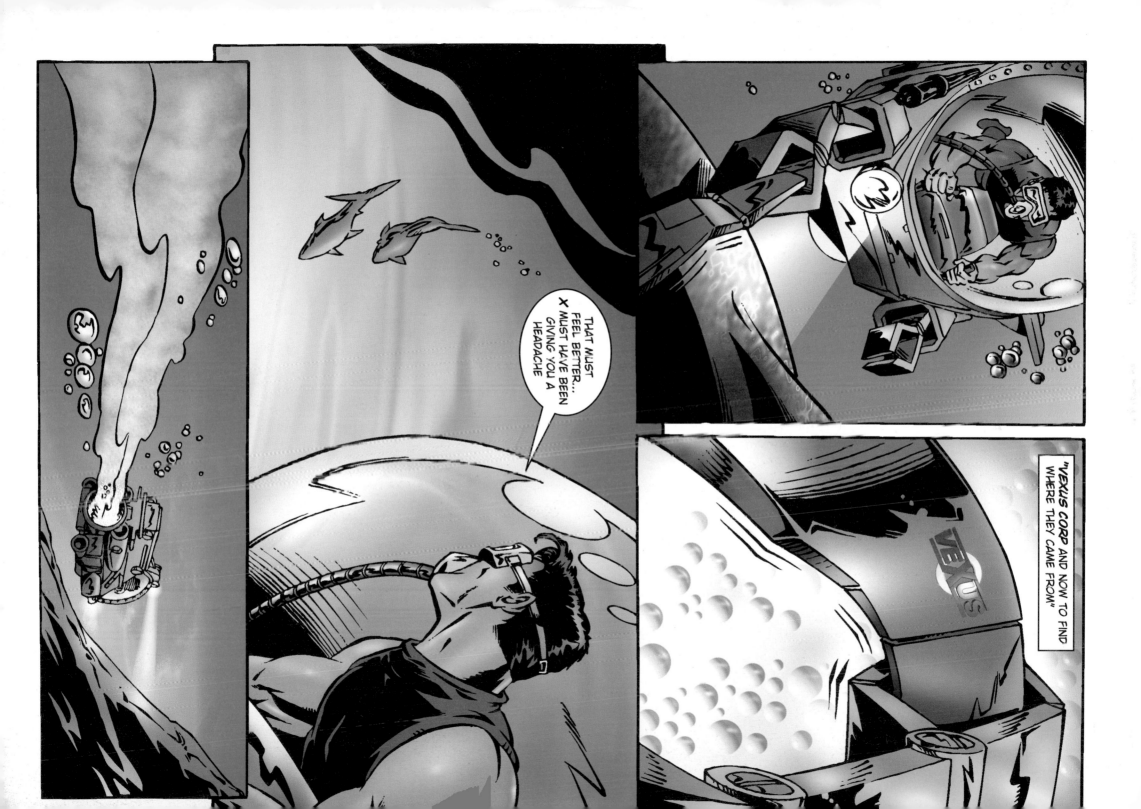

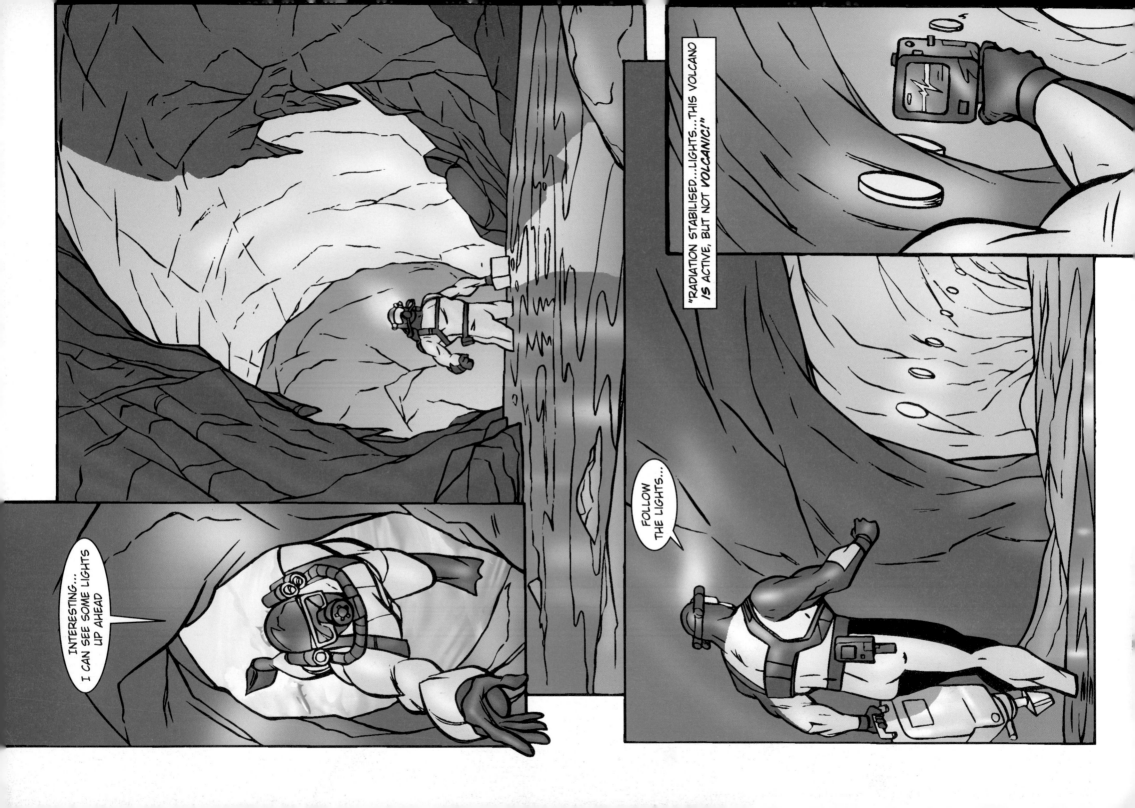

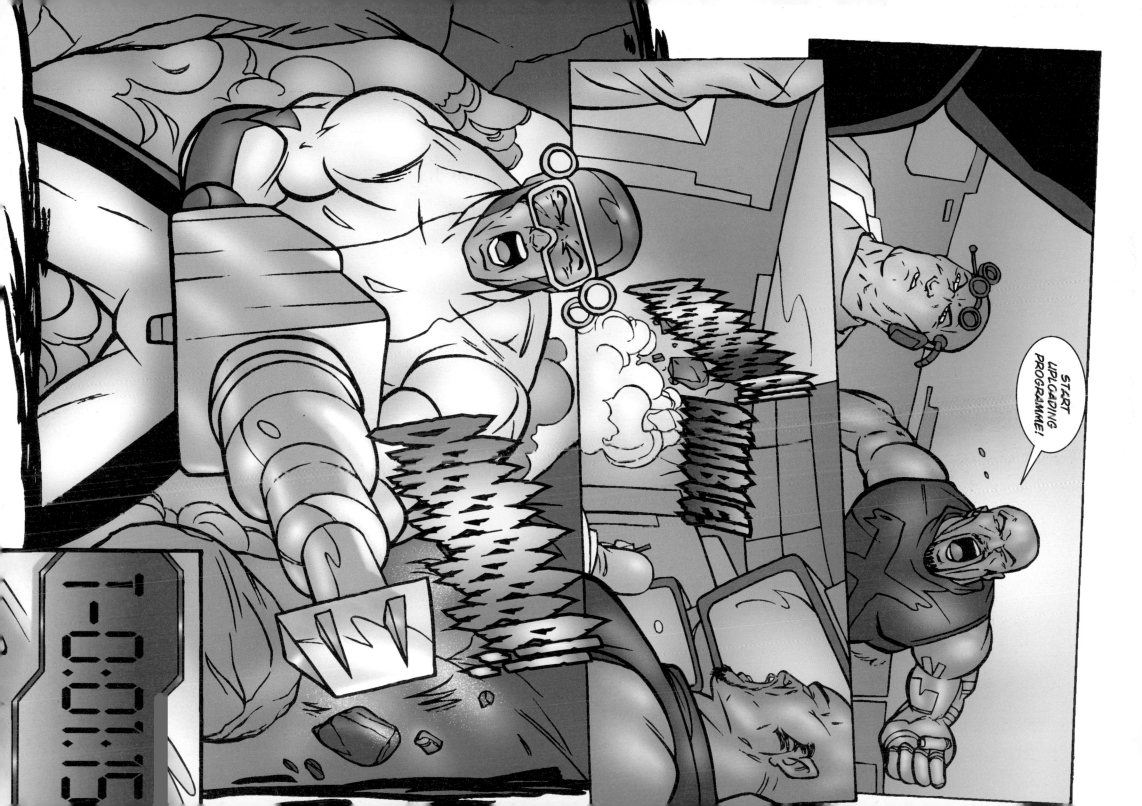

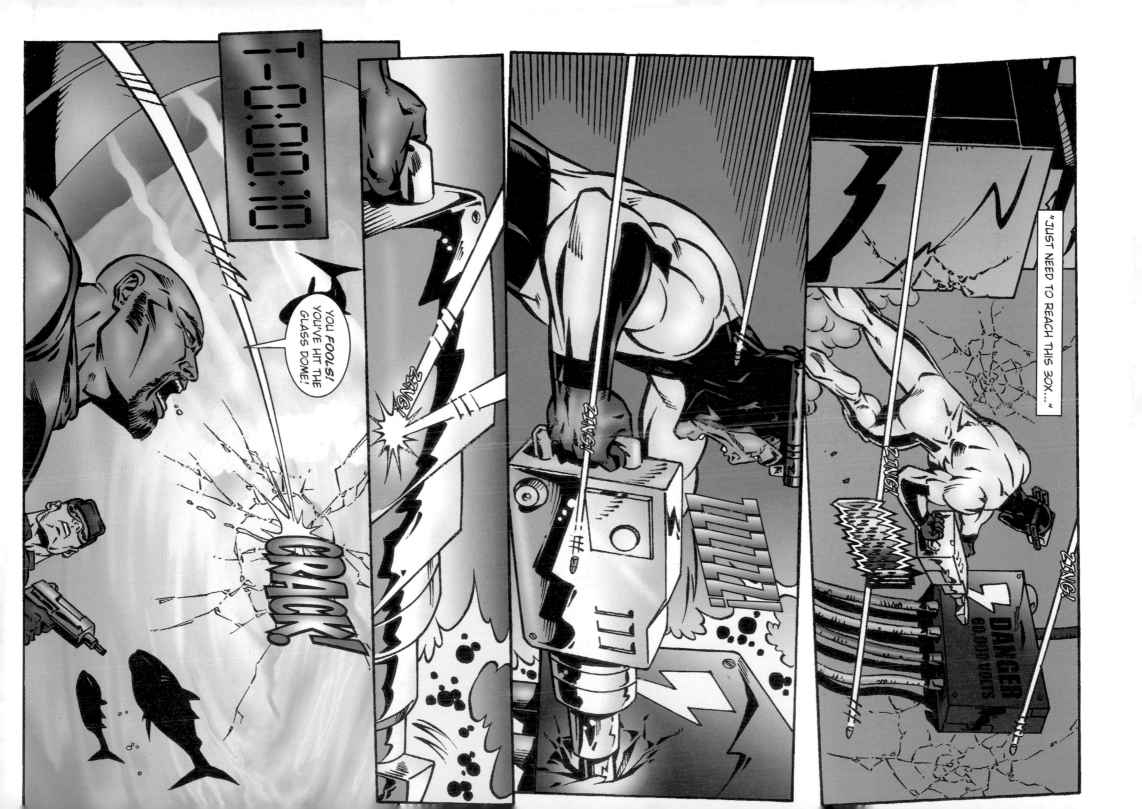

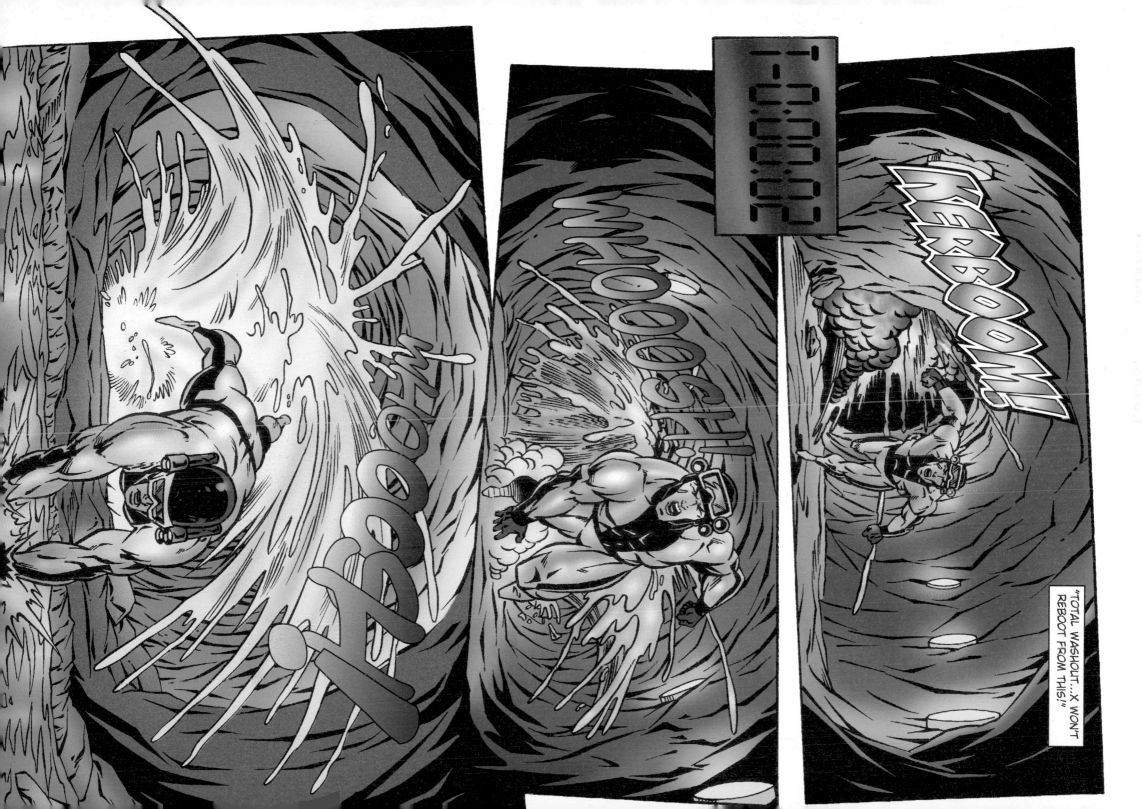

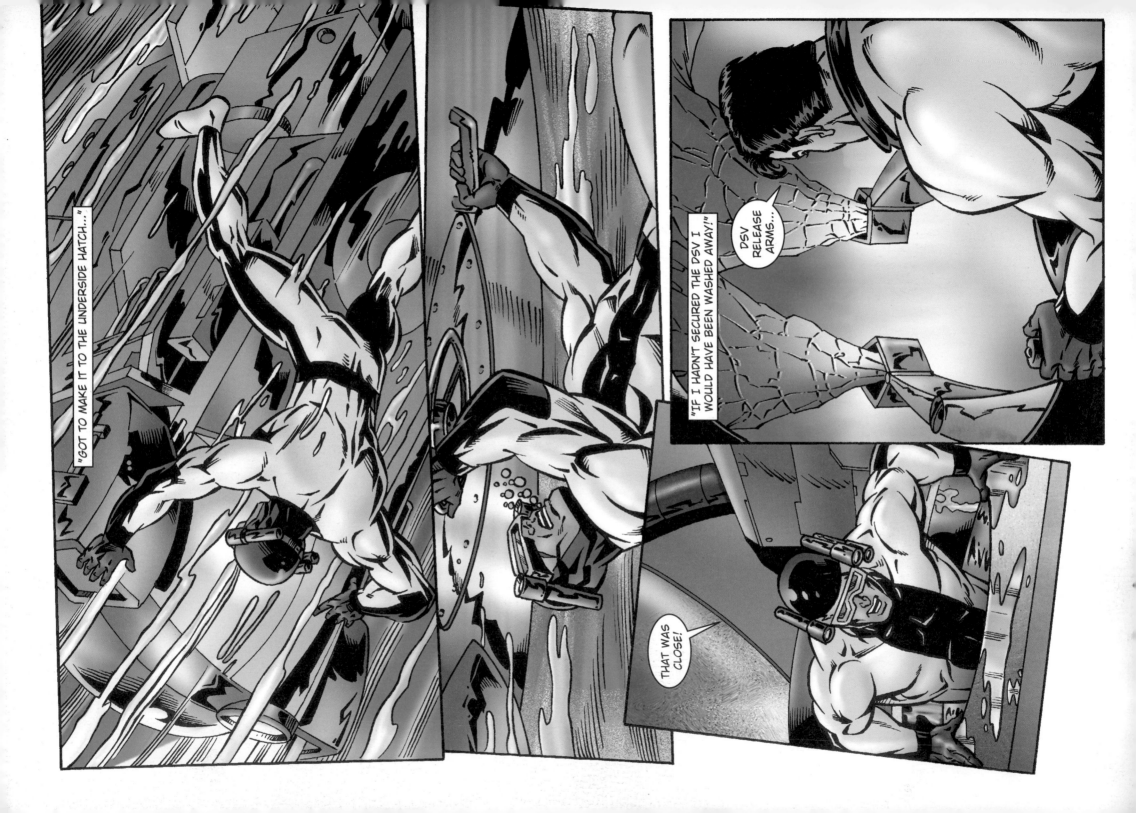

ACTION MAN

Mission Zone QUICK ACCESS CARD

Equipment QUICK ACCESS CARD

Reconnaissance QUICK ACCESS CARD

Mission Debriefing

Megabite

Action Man needs to debrief the European Defence Agency.

Can you help him extract the key information from the mission he has just completed.

Answer the questions by ticking the correct solution.

104

1. What caused the ships to go missing?
- A. Bermuda Triangle
- B. Hurricane
- C. Torpedoes

2. What are on the sharks?
- A. Computer control collars
- B. Barnacles
- C. Unknown

3. What is emitting from the volcano?
- A. Radiation
- B. Lava
- C. Smoke

4. How does Action Man get to the radiation source?
- A. Swim
- B. Drills through the wall
- C. Flies in

5. What finally stops the computer?
- A. Electricity being cut
- B. The seawater crashing in
- C. The sharks

6. How close is Dr.X to controlling the World?
- A. 1 hour
- B. 2 minutes
- C. 2 seconds

7. What happens to Dr.X?
- A. Action Man captures him
- B. He's frozen
- C. He is chased by his own sharks

Answers can be found on page 106

MIC

Design a new piece of equipment for Action Man to use underwater and when you have done it paste it into this box.

File Edit Type View Window Help

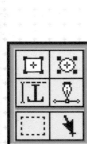

Mission Debriefing

EDA Equipment Designer

Answers from page 104:

1. What caused the ships to go missing?
   C. Torpedoes

2. What are on the sharks?
   A. Computer control collars

3. What is emitting from the volcano?
   A. Radiation

4. How does Action Man get to the radiation source?
   B. Drills through the wall

5. What finally stops the computer?
   B. The seawater crashing in

6. How close is Dr.X to controlling the World?
   C. 2 Seconds

7. What happens to Dr.X?
   C. He is chased by his own sharks

106

QUICK ACCESS CARD
Mission Zone

QUICK ACCESS CARD
Equipment

QUICK ACCESS CARD
Reconnaissance

ACTION MAN

ACTION MAN

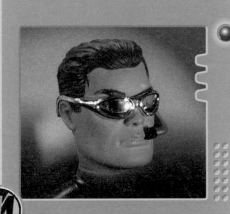

107

New Mail

INCOMING E-MAIL - SECURE LINK ENCODING

...1aiD GiC Dam kehCmCD ImD. 4bDahED Dam ame@ nBhf fI
DBECDml iomgDC q GhEel ghD jm ijem Dh lmnmiD lB.5 igl abC
FbCkhEC 5$1mif...pbC jhlI aiC ghD jmmg nhEgl# ieDahEoa
q+f CEBm DaiD Dam CaiBdC Gbee obFm abf i jboomB jbDm Daig
abC jiBd%smm@ i dmmg ehhdhED nhB igIDabgo CEC@bkbhEC igl
Bm@hBD jikd...ohhl tEkd bg Dam gmG fbeemggbEf.

...DECODING ENCRYPTION

...That was the closest yet. Without
the help from my trusted agents I
would not have been able to defeat
Dr.X and his viscous X-Team...

...His body has not been found,
although I'm sure that the sharks will
give him a bigger bite than his bark!

Keep a keen lookout for anything
suspicious and report back...

...Good Luck in the new millennium.

Action Man

...end transmission

EDA Secure Channel

Mission complete...Downloading new data...

INITIATE   COMMS.   MISSION   STATUS   AM2000PDA

MIC

ACTION MAN

Mission Zone	Equipment	Reconnaissance
QUICK ACCESS CARD	QUICK ACCESS CARD	QUICK ACCESS CARD

DR.X

Public Enemy Number One

Wanted Dr.X - Last seen in the Bermuda Triangle

The evil Dr.X has escaped justice once again.

Action Man and his fellow EDA Undercover Agents have foiled his latest evil scheme, but Dr.X has a long memory and has vowed to destroy Action Man and the EDA.

You can be sure he will be up to his usual tricks and sinister plots in 2000.

He cannot be allowed to go unpunished.

⊞ Psychological Profile - Dr.X

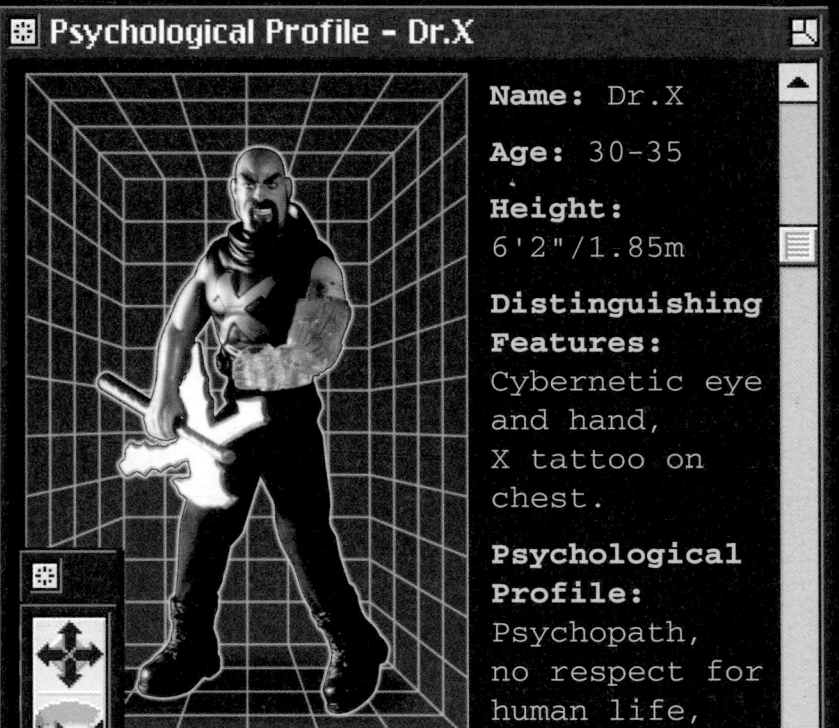

Name: Dr.X

Age: 30-35

Height: 6'2"/1.85m

Distinguishing Features: Cybernetic eye and hand, X tattoo on chest.

Psychological Profile: Psychopath, no respect for human life, highly intelligent.

Be on the lookout for Dr.X, you never know where he'll strike next

ACTION MAN

Your Photo

Title:

File   Edit   Type   View   Window   Help

New Mail

Action Man PDA2000 Mission Designer.

Copy the elements on this page to design your own PDA screens.

Using the mission briefs in this annual as a guide, design your own Mission and Equipment screens. Invent new Bad Guys and evil plots for Action Man to test his skill against.

EDA Secure Channel

Description:

INITIATE   COMMS.   MISSION   STATUS   *AM2000PDA*

MIC

Ultra Secret - Action Man Code Breaker

New Mail

INCOMING E-MAIL - SECURE LINK ENCODING
Message as follows:
>>From: EDA [http://www.actionman.com]

lBH aiC jmmg Cmmg iD Dam fbeemggbEf lhfm bg ehglhg

--- --- ---- ---- -- --- ---------- ---- -- -----

GaiD kig am jm @eiggbgo DabC Dbfm.

---- --- -- -- -------- ---- ----.

...end transmission

EDA Secure Channel

110

As an Undercover Operative for the EDA you will need to know how to use and break codes.

By comparing the letters that have already been decoded and by looking at the encrypted message on page 32, write out the alphabet and decode the message from the EDA.

Do not let this decoder fall into the hands of Dr.X or the X-Team.

Mission **ubCCbhg**

a		g		m		s	C	y	
b		h		n		t		z	J
c		i	b	o	h	u		.	.
d		j	c	p		v			
e		k		q		w			
f	n	l		r		x		M	u

Now create your own code.

a		g		m		s		y	Z
b		h		n		t	u	z	!
c		i		o		u	v	.	?
d		j		p		v			
e		k		q		w			
f	o	l		r		x			

EeDBi CmkBmD - ikDbhg fig khlm jBmidmB